Notes from a Feminist Killjoy

Notes from a Feminist Killjoy:

Essays on Everyday Life

Erin Wunker

BookThug
Toronto, 2016
Essais No. 2

SECOND PRINTING

The production of this book was made possible through the generous assistance of the Canada Council for the Arts and the Ontario Arts Council. BookThug also acknowledges the support of the Government of Canada through the Canada Book Fund and the Government of Ontario through the Ontario Book Publishing Tax Credit and the Ontario Book Fund.

LIBRARY AND ARCHIVES CANADA CATALOGUING IN PUBLICATION

(Essais ; no. 2)
Includes bibliographical references.

Issued in print and electronic formats.
ISBN 978-1-77166-256-7 (hardback)
ISBN 978-1-77166-257-4 (html)
ISBN 978-1-77166-258-1 (pdf)
ISBN 978-1-77166-259-8 (mobi)

Wunker, Erin, 1979–, author
    Notes from a feminist killjoy : essays on everyday life / Erin Wunker.

    1. Feminist theory. 2. Feminism. I. Title. II. Series: Essais (Toronto, ON.) ; 2

HQ1190.W85 2016   305.4201   C2016-904962-0   C2016-904963-9

PRINTED IN CANADA

Shelfie
A **bundled** eBook edition is available with the purchase of this print book.

CLEARLY PRINT YOUR NAME ABOVE IN UPPER CASE
Instructions to claim your eBook edition:
1. Download the Shelfie app for Android or iOS
2. Write your name in UPPER CASE above
3. Use the Shelfie app to submit a photo
4. Download your eBook to any device

Contents

Preface:
Letter to My Daughter

I don't know how to do this, wee one. Let's start there. Let's start with a blank page because despite the tiredness of the metaphor there is something beautiful and expansive and awe-inspiring about a blank page. Let's start with the page because starting with your little body in the world is too much for me right now. You are too tender. Let's start with the page.

Before you were born, when we called you Fetus Maximus because inscribing personhood onto the cluster of cells doing their work felt wrong, because the time would come (too quickly, too often) when the world would inscribe its expectations onto your little body, because I couldn't wrap my mind around you. Before you had a name and a gender and a heart that fluttered on a screen and dared me to disavow your possibility, I got a package in the mail in anticipation of you. In it, amongst the handmade quilt and the comically small slippers, was a book of envelopes. Each of the envelopes was labelled with an occasion: first week, first tooth, first day of school. The idea was to write you a letter for each of these occasions and to collect them in the book to be given to you when the time was right. I liked this idea. I liked the thought of telling you about yourself, of being your archive and your witness. But I didn't write a single letter. I couldn't. When I tried to start I didn't know how to begin. How could you be addressable as a "not-yet-you"? I didn't want to write my story as though it was yours. But here's the thing, babe, my story is your story. My body made your body, as bizarre and banal as that feels to write. We are each other's indexes at a cellular level. And so, my girl, these essays are first and foremost for you. Their partialities, their tenacious vulnerabilities, their fallibilities, and their insistent graspings at joy are my small attempts to show you that it's okay to try. It's okay to want to make your voice heard, and it's important to know your voice isn't the only one or the most important one. When I write about having a gendered body in the world, I think, now, about your tiny infant body. I think, now, about the only kind of prayer I utter with fervency: *May you be comfortable in your body and know it is yours. If your body doesn't fit you, may we find ways to make it yours. May your body only know pleasure and empowerment. May we give you the language to say yes, to say no. May the world be gentle with you. May you not lose that unselfconscious you-ness we hear from your crib when you wake up, singing. May you know the fierceness of strong friendships with women. May you be kind. May you feel held. May you write your own stories.*

Introduction:
Some Notes for You, Reading

I have a bitchy resting face.

You know what I mean: When I'm busy thinking or walk-ing or going about my daily business, my natural resting expression is one that reads to others as bitchy—or mean, or angry, or sad. Perfect strangers have told me to smile, cheer up, or simply not to look the way I do. Much to my chagrin, my automatic response is often to flash a grimacing smile. My reaction drives me bananas. I continue what I'm doing while thinking of witty (& not so witty) comebacks. I imagine crossing my eyes and sticking out my tongue. On a few occasions, though, I've had an inverse response to the automatic smile: I've given the happiness-seeking stranger the finger.

Why?

Not because the stranger necessarily deserves to be told

where to go (though let's be frank, often the stranger does). No, I've given people the finger or imagined doing so because there's something incredibly condescending about telling a woman to smile. Whether or not this smile-seeker is well meaning or a creep, there exists in much of the Western world a long and entrenched history of telling women how to think, feel, and act. And how to look. This history is complicated. It's varied. It shifts depending on your racial, gendered, ethnic, and class identity, but we can, for the sake of simplicity, call this the history of *patriarchal culture*.

★

In my own case, I had to train myself out of that phony smile, which is like a nervous tic on every teenage girl. And this meant that I smiled rarely, for in truth, when it came down to real smiling, I had less to smile about. My "dream" action for the women's liberation movement: a smile boycott, at which declaration all women would instantly abandon their "pleasing" smiles, henceforth smiling only when something pleased them.[1]

★

Essais. That's the name of the series this book is published in—*essais*. This book is a record of me trying to write about feminism at the interstices of critical and literary theory, pop culture, and feminist thinking. At the intersection of those

---

1. Shulamith Firestone, *The Dialectic of Sex: The Case for Feminist Revolution* (New York: Morrow, 1970) 90.

methods and epistemological routes is me. I'm writing in the *I*. I'm inserting myself in a long and varied tradition of women and other marginalized people working from a situated position of knowledge. I'm also busting in on and turning over tables within the other long tradition of speaking subjects who use *I* without thinking twice about the privilege that entails. Me, I think twice, three, even four times about that privilege.

Who do I think I am?

★

In April 2016, the Canadian magazine *The Walrus* published an article by Jason Guriel entitled "I Don't Care About Your Life: Why Critics Need to Stop Getting Personal In Their Essays."[2] In the essay, Guriel laments the hybridization of the confessional and the critical forms. The confessional—shorthand, in Guriel's article, for shitty, navel-gazing writing—dilutes what might otherwise be pure critique.

(Arguments for purity make me cringe, usually, unless of course we are talking about water quality.)

Despite my training as an academic, which taught me that I could be a cool and impartial professional reader, writer, teacher, and critic, this article got under my skin. Reading

2. Jason Guriel, "I Don't Care about Your Life," *The Walrus* 14 Apr 2016 <https://thewalrus.ca/i-dont-care-about-your-life/>.

it, I felt acutely uncomfortable. I felt seen (called out?) in a way that was vulnerable-making. It felt as though he was taking aim at writers who inspire me enormously, at me, and at the deliberate stylistic and genre choices writers make. I felt all the work I do to situate my own knowledge—as a teacher, as a reader, as a writer—was suddenly and impudently invalidated.

I don't know J.G., but the Internet tells me he might like baseball, and the Blue Jays in particular, so we do have that much in common... And yet...

I was reminded of a similar feeling of vulnerability that occurred during the first week of graduate school: I was sitting outside smoking with a bunch of my fellow (male) students and they all got to talking about how much they hated Margaret Atwood. I didn't hate Margaret Atwood. Nor did I hate her writing. And, as I sat there listening to these people talk confidently about how she was a hack writer and a bitch, I got quiet. I didn't speak up. I most certainly didn't stick up for Margaret (she doesn't need my help, I thought), and I definitely didn't talk about my favourite writer at the time (Eden Robinson, in case you're wondering). Instead I sat, smoking, listening, and nodding like one of those dashboard bobbleheads.

*

I'm not really known for keeping my opinion to myself these days, so why did I then?

And why did Guriel's article bother me so much?

*

Does. Why *does* it bother me so much?

*

About a week after Guriel's article was published, Mandy Len Catron published a response entitled "You Should Care About My Life: The First-Person Pronoun Isn't Trivial, It's Essential."[3] She says so many things that get to the heart of what's wrong with Guriel's stance.

Like: What do you mean by conflating the confessional with the narcissistic and lazy?

Or: Who is privileged enough not to see that all writing is deeply and inherently coloured by our subjective and individuated experiences?

And that so many writers— including Ta-Nehisi Coates, Timothy Tu, James Baldwin—write from the *I* perspective in radical ways because their experiences—their own I-positions—are marginalized.

Yes, I nodded as I read. Yes.

---

3. Mandy Len Catron, "You Should Care about My Life: The First-Person Pronoun Isn't Trivial, It's Essential," *The Walrus* 20 Apr 2016 <https://thewalrus.ca/you-should-care-about-my-life/>.

*

No mention of women in either article, though.

No mention of women, save to imply that I-writing is femi-nized (because the confessional as a genre is a feminized genre save for the outlier/insider Robert Lowell, pretty much. Anne Sexton, Sylvia Plath, Robert Lowell. Those poets who crack worlds open with their honesty. I learned in school to mistrust their realness and read it as excessive feminine blathering. I learned to read their writing through their suicides as evidence of some sort of weakness. Their poetry became a kind of cautionary tale about exposing too much of yourself. I exaggerate, but that's the point, isn't it?).[4]

*

What gets under my skin about the *Walrus* article, then, is that it's one in a long and tedious line of literary dismiss-als of the vital necessity of being able to say *I* in a public space... and of having your own authority over your life trusted. Who gets to say *I* without having to shore up that utterance with justification for the right to speak? To exist? Not women. Not women of colour. Not people of colour. Not queer people. Not trans people. Not differently abled

---

4. Actually, I don't exaggerate. See Karissa LaRocque's "Easily Dismissed as a Mirror Image" (<http://gutsmagazine.ca/blog/easily-dismissed-mirror-image>) for a strong introduction to the ways in which confessional writ-ers—especially Sylvia Plath—have been infantilized.

people. Not a hell of a lot of people, as it turns out. So why is the *I* so easily dismissed?

Because, I think, it's risky. For the speaker. For the status quo.

*

I'm taking a risk here.

*

When I started writing this book I thought I was going to write a handbook. A how-to on Sara Ahmed's concept of being a feminist killjoy, that irreverent figure who lights a match and joyfully flicks it into the dry hull of patriarchal culture.

There were going to be key terms and quizzes and ten easy steps.

*

Turns out, there are more than ten steps.

*

Turns out, this isn't a handbook.

*

Why do I feel so invested in the *I*? I asked my partner this one evening as we sat in a small, dark café off the square where we were living in Spain for a few precious weeks. It's a cliché to say that we are rarely out alone together these post-bébé days, but it is also true, and in those rare moments I can feel us both reaching towards each other, our once more familiar way of thinking and being together in public spaces, of talking and thinking, and falling contemplatively silent.

That's hyperbole, of course. On that evening, I don't actually know what he was thinking or feeling. All I can described is what I saw and felt and observed from my own corner of the tiny table.

And that's it, I realized, as he took up my question and unspooled it with me. The *I* is an interstice, not an intersection. An opening. Not "relatable" (a quality our freshest students so lamentably look for in almost everything), but a possibility. *I* invites observation at the level of the personal and the intimate without allowing the observer to mistake the observed for anything other than what it is: individuated. Familiar, sometimes, yes. Radically other, often. But *I* is an invitation to listen. It is an invitation to follow one body's thinking, one possibility's path.

In the language of my academic training, as a student of the 1990s and 2000s, *I* is the reason that standpoint epistemology matters. We need to learn how to approach the experiences—gendered, raced, classed—of others as contextual. We need to learn how to approach our own experiences as contextual. And *I* is a wonderfully messy shorthand for all those blurred borders of experience.

The intersection of the personal and the critical—the theoretical, the "hard"—is crucial for me and for this book. *Creative nonfiction is... interesting prose that bears witness to fact, life, and the problematics of having a body in spacetime.*[5]

★

When I started writing this book, I didn't think I was a writer. I thought I was a teacher. After all, I had spent nearly a decade teaching in post-secondary institutions. I had written a doctoral dissertation and been given the funny-looking hat. I had been a feminist-academic blogger for almost five years. I chaired the board of the Canadian Women in the Literary Arts, which is a national not-for-profit organization focused on fostering representational justice in Canadian literary culture.

What I mean is, I felt that I knew how to write, I just was not *a writer*.

★

I think, now, that there are questions to be asked about

---

5. Maggie Nelson, "Maggie Nelson's Six Nonfiction Writers," *Vela: Written By Women* n.d. <http://velamag.com/bookmarked-maggie-nelsons-six-nonfiction-writers/>.

access, ownership, and agency. I think, now, that claiming space and having a place at the table of Big Ideas and Important Thinking are not the same thing. I think, as I write myself into being a writer, that there's a lot of work to be done on many different levels. Figuring out where and how I stand, myself, seems crucial in order to try to stand with others who are affected differently by aggressions of misogyny, racism, homophobia, transphobia, ableism, class, and, and, and...

And then the problem of audience came up: Who is the audience for this book? I asked myself. I was also asked by others. And I wasn't sure. I couldn't tell you. Not in a few words, like we're taught. There was no elevator speech ready.

★

It would seem that I am writing this book for everyone. And also for myself. And for the wee one who is napping as I write. The risk, of course, is to be called (or to be) navel-gazing. I'll take it. I'll take that risk.

The act of writing is "bodying forth" another iteration of me, of my thinking, of how I'm able to move through the world. It is another iteration of how I see others and how I see myself.

★

So here is what I found myself explaining to myself when I was thinking through why the *Walrus* piece bothered me and why I worried about my lack of defense of Atwood and how I would try to talk to my extended family about this book you're reading and how I would try to talk to my students about feminism. Here is what I found myself thinking: this whole "*I* is a feminized and therefore narcissistic and less-than position from which to write" thing is a denizen of patriarchal culture.

And what is patriarchal culture, Erin? I can hear my dad or my first-year students asking, albeit in different tones of voice.

(Don't assume my dad is the one with his eyebrow raised, skeptical. Don't assume my students are, either.)

Here's the start of an essay—an *essai*, a trial, attempt, endeavour—that reaches towards some answers.

*

Patriarchal culture is by definition a culture in which masculinity—in people and in things—is privileged as inherently foundational to other states of being. In a patriarchal culture, systems, institutions, and social interactions reinforce this hierarchy. When you live in a patriarchal culture, as in any culture, you begin learning its rules and regulations, as well as the way you fit into them, almost immediately. It's important to note that patriarchal culture is not an equitable culture. It's unfair for women and women-identified people, and it's also unfair for men, though these unfairnesses are not the same, nor do all people experience them the same way. Like any culture or way of being, patriarchal culture appears to be inscrutable. It is so entrenched in our psyches and our ways of moving through the world that it seems impossible to change.

I am most acutely aware of this entrenchment when I catch myself in the midst of an automatic grimace/smile, hating myself for responding by rote and hating the stranger for demanding a rote response. My responses feel programmed at gut-level. They feel unimpeachable. It's intensely difficult to reprogram oneself. And who even knows where to begin deprogramming a stranger, much less a series of interlocking systems that lead to an automatic and regretted smile?

Yet, as the science fiction writer Ursula K. LeGuin points out, totalizing systems are built to appear inscrutable: *We live in capitalism. Its power seems inescapable. So did the divine right of kings. Any human power can be resisted and changed by human beings.*[6] The first step to resisting inequity and changing it must be learning to see it. And seeing that unequal power catches us each up differently.

*

When, as a younger person, I learned that in many profes-

---

6. Ursula LeGuin, "Speech in Acceptance of the National Book Foundation Medal for Distinguished Contribution to American Letters," 19 Nov 2014 <https://www.youtube.com/watch?v=Et9Nf-rsALk>

sions in Canada women were paid seventy-seven cents for every dollar a man is paid for the same work, I was shocked.[7] How was this possible? *Now?* Wasn't wage differentiation a thing of the past?

In March of 2016, *Huffington Post Canada* published a piece entitled "Canada's Gender Pay Gap: Why Canadian Women Still Earn Less Than Men." Its author, Arti Patel, cites studies from Statistics Canada that measure the current wage discrepancy at seventy-three cents on the dollar. In other words, women in Canada who are working full-time earn on average seventy-three cents for every dollar a man working full-time in Canada earns. That's to say that the wage gap has increased since I first learned about it. And as Patel points out, *these numbers are even lower for Indigenous and women of colour.*[8] So no, wage differentiation is not a thing of the past.

What the actual fuck?

The answer—to this fact, to my F-bomb, to why I didn't see the wage discrepancy before I learned about it in a university classroom—is, of course, like so many other structural inequities with long and violent histories (think rac-

7. See, for example, Cara Williams's report for Statistics Canada: "Economic Well-being," Dec 2010 <http://www.statcan.gc.ca/pub/89-503-x/2010001/article/11388-eng.pdf>.

8. Arti Patel, "Canada's Gender Pay Gap: Why Canadian Women Still Earn Less Than Men," The Huffington Post 8 Mar 2016 <http://www.huffingtonpost.ca/2016/03/08/canada-gender-pay-gap_n_9393924.html>.

ism, colonialism, homophobia): complicated. Why didn't I "see" this wage discrepancy before I was eighteen or twenty years old? In part because it's a hidden facet—and fact—of patriarchal culture and also in part because I hadn't been directly confronted with the wage gap. Moreover, not only did I lack the language for articulating inequitable power systems and for naming my place in them; I also lacked the experiential awareness that many other people experience earlier for a variety of reasons I'll go on to discuss. What I mean is this: my family was middle-class. Both my parents worked, though my mom stopped working as a cardiac nurse when I was about five years old. She stayed home with me, dad worked.

She stayed home.

As if child care and household labour aren't work. But I didn't *see* or understand this subtle division as a gendered division of labour. Moreover, given that my family is white as well as middle-class, I didn't see my parents experience the additional micro- and macro-aggressions of racism that affect how much and, indeed, whether, people get paid fair wages for their labour. I lacked experiential awareness. This lack of mine was demonstrated in my inability to see these hidden, though obvious things—these open secrets of the gendered and racialized wage gap. Naming the lack and speaking the open secrets are some of the tasks of a feminist killjoy.

*

It occurs to me that being a feminist killjoy is a more than a full-time job.

*

But wait. I realize that before I sketch out just a few of the myriad ways in which patriarchal culture creates and perpetuates inequity, I need to talk about why feminism is important.

*

The first step to shifting patriarchal culture into something more fair and equitable is to recognize the imperative and urgent need for feminism. Yes, still. Yes, now. Yes, in the first few decades of the 2000s. Yes, in North America. Yes, to form coalitions. Yes, across class lines. Yes, across gendered lines. Yes, in different iterations to speak to different people. Yes, in conjunction with anti-racism. Yes, in cooperation with policy reform. Yes, for people with children. Yes, for people without children. Yes, we need it. Yes.

*

Feminist: one who recognizes that the material conditions of contemporary life are built on inequities of gender, race, and class. One who recognizes that patriarchal culture is inherently coercive and stifling for women and other Others. One who works to make those inequities visible and one who works to tear them down. One who recognizes the enormity of the task. One who keeps working.

*

We need feminism as a way of thinking, as a way of being in the world, as a methodology for teaching children, as much as we need it as a methodology for enacting policy changes at the federal level. But the term "feminist" still pulls many people up short. It's at once antiquated (weren't they the bra-burners of the 1960s? Answer: *yes* and *no*) *and* too politically risky [aren't they the left-wing, angry man-haters? Answer: *yes, sometimes (but we need to ask what conditions exist that make this possible) and, no, not necessarily*]. Feminism is complicated, sure, but throwing out the term simply because it's freighted means throwing out the histories and struggles that have brought the term forward. So how do we both reinvigorate our understanding of the history of feminist activism *and* come to terms with the ongoing and urgent need for feminist consciousness in this not-so-new millennium?

*

When I started this book, I wanted to write something unimpeachable. Something so clear and objective, it could be a little dictionary or translation phrase book for how to speak a feminist language and live a feminist life. I wanted what many other writers—*the many-gendered mothers of my heart*—had already written.[9] I wanted *A Room of One's Own*, *Sister Outsider, Willful Subjects, Islands of Decolonial Love*. I wanted *Feminism is for Everybody* and *The Dream of a Common Language*. I wanted *No Language is Neutral*.[10]

I wanted books that had already been written by people whose experiences of moving through the world are different—often radically so—from mine.

*

I got stuck.

*

I read some more.

*

I remembered that I tell my students that reading and writing are attempts at joining conversations, making new ones, and, sometimes, shifting the direction of discourse.

*

---

9. That's Maggie Nelson in her brilliant work of auto-theory, *The Argonauts* (Minneapolis: Graywolf Press, 2015), quoting Dana Ward (p.86).

10. These books were written by Virginia Woolf, Audre Lorde, Sara Ahmed, Leanne Betasamosake Simpson, bell hooks, Adrienne Rich, and Dionne Brand, respectively.

I sat down at my computer again.

*

When I began this book, I was pregnant. When I began writing again, I'd given birth. This matters to me, but it needn't matter to you in the same way. What's important to know, for now, is that something had shifted between my first attempt to write this text and my next one. Something subtle. I loosened my grip on some things (I'll never write those books that hold my heart and shape my thinking), and I tightened my grip on others (I can talk with them, those books, those thinkers, you.)

This book is a collection of attempts. Notes *for* conversations, notes *from* conversations. It is a book that uses some critical theory and some cultural references to offer concrete suggestions for manoeuvring through shared experiences and spaces. It is also a partial book that bears the limitations of its author. Me. She of the bitchy resting face.

*

This book is divided into four main sections. After this introduction, there's a chapter on rape culture, then one on friendships, and, finally, a chapter on feminist mothering. I wrote the chapters one at a time without knowing, initially, where they were going. I call the chapters *notes* because that's the form they took. My writing happened in small bursts, on what seemed like little Post-it notes of time. As

I've mentioned, our daughter was born just after I started writing, and by the time she was six months old, I was... six months behind schedule. My partner was teaching what is more than a full load of courses for an academic, and I was teaching two courses as a sessional. We didn't have child care in the fall, and in the winter of this writing, we had a total of eight hours a week of help from two wonderful humans, N. and C.

This all matters because the conditions in which I was working shaped this book profoundly. Not only have I written in snippets of time—in the oh-my-god-it-is-too-early morning; while bébé was napping; in the late evening; in the tiny moments of time I might have been spending with my partner—I also wrote in small chunks. I wrote, I sent my brilliant editor my words, and she'd think with me on them. We wrote notes to one another in the margins of my thinking, and these notes—the questions, suggestions, and proddings—got incorporated into my writing.

To J., then: This book was a thinking with you. Thank you for becoming friends with me and with my thinking. Thank you for nudging this book into being.

I also wrote notes to a few trusted friends. R., especially, helped me think through rape culture and how to talk about it. She taught me that "victim" and "survivor" are terms that might better be traded for "endurance." Living in rape culture is an exercise in endurance and enduring. Thank you, R.

So, yeah. Notes. Notations of moments in time. Notes from my memories of conversations. Notes in the margins of other writers' thinking. Notes written to my daughter. Notes written to you.

The chapters bring together my training as an academic, a reader, and a blogger. There's theory, pop culture, and me. I open with a chapter on rape culture because gender-based violence permeates our world. When I was writing the first draft of this introduction, the trial in Canada of the former media-darling Jian Ghomeshi was in process. While I'm revising, I'm reading about the ways that cultures of toxic masculinity emerge: the Stanford rapist, his father's apologia for *twenty minutes of action* (i.e., raping a woman while she was passed out behind a dumpster).[11] While I am revising this, *Pulse*: forty-nine beautiful humans massacred for being on a dance floor in a gay bar. Forty-nine people, most of whom were people of colour. As I revise this, Alton Sterling. Philando Castille. Dallas. Baton Rouge. Turkey. And as Rebecca Solnit writes in *Men Explain Things To Me*, the common denominator of these kinds of violences is that they are not being enacted by women. Patriarchal culture is no good for anyone.

So I open with rape culture; I wade in. It was hard to write, mostly because what I have written is so partial, so subjective. But I start there. We start there.

11. Mary Elizabeth Williams, "Stanford Rapist's Father Issues a Despicable Plea for Leniency: 'A Steep Price to Pay for 20 Minutes of Action,'" *Salon* 6 Jun 2016 <http://bit.ly/1VHWYyr>.

The next chapter is about friendship. A feminist killjoy needs friends. And friendship is a radical act. In this chapter I think about friendships among women, the radicalities these friendships enact, and some of the ways in which mainstream culture teaches us to mistrust friendships between women. The chapter closes with a recounting of one of the most vital acts of literary friendship I have read.

The final chapter is about mothering and feminism. More specifically, it is about coming into myself as a mother who was already a feminist. It is about the ways in which the labours of child care are gendered, still. And it is about learning (again) to ask for help. It is also a bit of a love story. I fall in love with the kiddo and with the new and complicated contradictions and challenges of being a feminist killjoy who is also a mom.

Finally, there's a postscript. What note is complete without a p.s.? Not this one. Here, I think about refusal as a feminist act and try to leave you with a sense of how my own work as a feminist killjoy operates at the interstices of my own identity as feminist/teacher/friend/ally/mother.

★

Again, the personal pronoun *I* is crucial; it's a site from which we can take stock, take responsibility, and take space if space is needed. The feminist scholar Donna Haraway argues that human perception is limited and partial, and thus we need a term that can act as a placeholder indicating that partiality; she offers the term *situated knowledge*. Situating yourself enacts the deliberate practice of locating your own identity and experiences as coming from somewhere and being mediated by certain things such as your race, gender, and class. Laying these things out for yourself locates your way of being in the world—your knowledge—within larger systems of knowing. It also lays bare our own myopic positionalities: we are short-sighted when it comes to the experiences of others. Example: Remember when Beyoncé's "Formation" dropped and suddenly white listeners were all *its so political! She's into Black Power now!* as though there's not a long, complex history of Blackness, resistance, performance, and racism? History *matters*. If you want to understand Beyoncé's performance, then you need to do the work of learning about Black experience in America and in the world. Of Black women's experiences. Of the multiplicities of history, of resistance, of performance, and of racism. Just downloading *Lemonade* doesn't do it. All those white folks who were surprised by her politics? They had never been in a position that required them to think through, learn, or listen to the histories of Black experience. For real.

This surprise is an example of just one of the ways myopias work.

Situating your knowledge means that you have to start recognizing the ways in which your knowledge has been shaped—for better or worse—by external social forces. It also means opening yourself to the truth that you don't have access to every experience.

*

A question I keep asking myself—to keep me honest, to keep me working—is how we can navigate the tension between the specific and the general that this work of situating oneself introduces? After all, even if you share my background, ethnicity, and class, we may not share the same politics, experiences, and ethos. Still, this is a starting point, one that makes me vulnerable to you. I hope that vulnerability opens a space.

*

Here, then, is some information that helps to situate me: I am a cis-gendered, able-bodied woman. I am white. English is my first language, though I speak French and Italian relatively well (and better when I've had a glass of wine). I was raised by middle-class parents, who were raised by working-class parents and middle-class parents. I am a university-educated, PhD-holding, sometimes-teacher of literature, culture, and Canadian Studies. At the time of writing this book, I'm unemployed because there is a crisis in post-secondary education and there are not enough jobs. I have more than ten years of post-secondary teaching experience and have taught at four universities in three provinces. I was born in Canada to an American mother and a Canadian father. I grew up between Ontario and rural North Carolina. I've lived in several countries and most of the provinces in Canada. Currently, I live in Nova Scotia, where I came for contract academic work in 2009. I love

Atlantic Canada, and my partner and I will try to stay if we can find steady work. I live with a man and a baby and a dog; the dog chose me, the man and I chose each other, and we decided to have the baby. Despite our seeming appearances, our family is a queer one. We pass, which is its own kind of complicated privilege. I have self-identified as a feminist for about a decade.

In short, though work is scant and paid work has been hard for me to come by, in most identity categories of my life I move through the world with a great deal of relative privilege. Because of my experiences of unearned privilege—which I'd flag as my cis-gender, whiteness, class, and language of birth—it took me a while to learn what a feminist killjoy is, why I was one, why I wanted to commit to being a better and more active one, and why the world needs more feminist killjoys. Let me be clear: I am not apologizing for my identity, but I am trying to be direct about how factors beyond my control—my race, language of birth, gender identification—have fit more neatly into contemporary patriarchal culture's narrow parameters than those factors that other people may experience. In other words, I have to work at "seeing" certain kinds of my own privilege, because privilege often blinds. You may have a very different experience than mine, and that matters immensely. But I can only speak with authority for myself.

Situating oneself is a crucial early step in becoming a feminist killjoy.

★

This book takes its title from postcolonial feminist critic Sara Ahmed's blog, *feministkilljoys*, and it is deeply informed by all of her work. Reading Ahmed is, for me, an experience of reaching across the space that vulnerability can open. It is an act of listening hard and learning. It is work.

The tagline for Ahmed's blog reads, *Killing joy as a world making project*. The statement is aggressive, and it is hopeful. It's a paradox not unlike the figure of the feminist killjoy. Or a book of notes and essays on being a feminist killjoy. If you are a person concerned with the state of the world, enraged and discouraged by inequity, and fuelled by the desire to *do something*, chances are you're already a feminist killjoy. You may even find that recognizing the ways in which "killing joy is a world making project" can, in fact, be emboldening. After all, if what *is* isn't working for many of us, the working towards what *could be* is an exercise in hope.

Let's not pretend that being hopeful is an easy or straightforward pursuit. *Hope can be a fracturing, even a traumatic thing to experience,* writes Eve Kosofsky Sedgwick.[12] Experiencing hope may bring oxygen to a stifled set of lungs, but hope also brings the realization that if something else is possible, then the stifling wasn't necessary or inevitable. Experiencing hope means running the risk of a kind of

---

12. Eve Kosofsky Sedgwick, *Touching Feeling: Affect, Pedagogy, Performativity* (Durham: Duke UP, 2003) 146.

crushing disappointment and agitated torpor that Lauren Berlant refers to as *cruel optimism*.[13] So yes, it's complicated to be a hopeful feminist killjoy, complicated and necessary.

It's not necessarily easy or intuitive to identify yourself as a feminist, much less to take up the mantle of a feminist killjoy. At least, it wasn't for me. I remember sitting in a classroom as a first-year PhD student, listening to my professor talk about the history of feminism in North America. She asked us to self-identify as feminists on a piece of paper. I wrote something to the effect of "I'm not a feminist because I think women are equal now, but I am concerned about the ongoing effects of racism and class disparity." I felt pretty smug in my own self-knowledge. There I was, aware that I had accessed the achievements of previous feminist work simply by being in a classroom and not having my right to be there questioned. Sure, I knew that feminism had been important, but mostly I felt that I had missed the major events of North American feminist history. I grew up with the right to vote, as did my mother and my grandmother. I was reaping the benefits of the second-wave fight for equal rights (or so I thought). And I was just a bit too young to have participated in the Riot Grrrl movement, though the music and words of folks like Kathleen Hanna gave me the uncanny sense that all was not quite right in all that I thought was (al)right. And yet. For the most part I felt pretty self-assured.

---

13. Lauren Berlant, *Cruel Optimism* (Durham: Duke UP, 2011).

*

Smugness in one's own self-knowledge is often a signal that you don't know as much as you think you do.

*

I was wrong about not needing feminism, just as I was wrong to think feminism had achieved all of its aims.[14] Grievously wrong. In fact, I see now some of the ways that my answer bespoke my need for feminism, my need to understand multi-faceted feminism, and my need to recognize and reflect upon my own privilege and the myopias that come with it. For as much as I'm loath to admit it, sitting there in that classroom in the early 2000s, I did not immediately recognize my own whiteness as a privilege that made me feel that the classroom was a natural space for me. Nor did I recognize that my cis-gender—that is, my gender identification matching up with how people *read* my gender in the street—was its own unearned pass card into relatively fluid movement through the world. Why didn't I recognize those privileges? First, my own relative privilege meant I hadn't had to fight for my own legitimacy in the world in the ways that others are and have been fighting for for generations. Second, I didn't yet recognize the ways in

---

14. The singular "its" is a problem here, as I will go on to discuss. Feminism isn't singular, though its mainstream narrative has historically been myopic in its focus on whiteness, middle-classness, and heteronormativity. For the sake of grammatical simplicity, I will continue to refer to feminism in the singular for the moment.

which I was already entangled in and internalizing the rules and regulations of a heteronormative, patriarchal, and racist social order. Put simply, I didn't see how inequality was affecting me on a daily basis, in part because of my relative privilege and, in another part, because I had been taught to internalize and make normal the rules of the system. (Picture me flashing that automatic, grimacing smile...) For example, it didn't occur to me that the near-universal message to women, "don't walk alone at night," was in any way a feminist issue. Of course I shouldn't walk home alone at night, I thought. That's how you get raped (mind you, I stopped thinking this made sense when I actually was raped by an acquaintance at a party full of people...). I didn't understand that my own internalization of fear, guilt, and victim-blaming was in fact a means of keeping the status quo. The status quo: also known as patriarchal culture? Well, friends, the status quo isn't equality. Not for women, not for women-identified people, not for women of colour, not for queer women, not for working class women, not for homeless women or women sex-workers, and not even for men. In other words, these few internalizations I've noted are symptomatic of growing up in a patriarchal culture.

Another key symptom of patriarchal culture that requires feminist intervention is our inability to see different instances of inequity as connected. For example, while this book is made up of a series of essays on feminism that speak from my point of view using that personal pronoun *I*, I think a

great deal about racism, classism, and homophobia throughout the essays. Why? Because while my lens is focused on
developing a discussion of feminism and becoming a feminist killjoy, it's impossible to do an accurate job of this without underscoring the ways in which fighting other inequities
intersects with feminist aims.

*

My feminism is intersectional, in other words.

*

Intersectional feminism is a feminist methodology—a way
of being, thinking, and moving through the world—that
takes into account the multiple factors that shape an individual's or a group's lived experience. For example: if we
take as a common denominator the category "woman"
without an intersectional approach to feminism, we *might*
be tempted to suggest that *all women everywhere have certain
shared experiences.* And then let's augment this claim with
Hortense Spiller's observation that when people talk about
"women" in feminist circles, they usually means "white
women."[15] An intersectional approach, however, takes into
account the ways in which different oppressive conditions—

---

15. Hortense Spillers writes about this in the chapter entitled "Interstices: A
Small Drama of Words" in *Black, White, and in Color: Essays on American Literature and Culture* (Chicago: University of Chicago Press, 2003) 152–175. [First
published in Carol Vance, ed. *Pleasure and Danger: Exploring Female Sexuality*
(New York: Pandora/HarperCollins, 1984).]

sexism, ableism, homophobia, racism, transphobia, classism and so on—are interconnected. We cannot talk about one system in utter isolation from another. The lived experience of a working-class white woman is not identical to the lived experience of an upper-class Black woman or a middle-class trans woman or a woman student who is paraplegic. As legal scholar Kimberlé Crenshaw points out, we would do well to employ an intersectional lens when looking at different systems of oppression. An intersectional feminist approach takes time and vigilance and practice. It requires that we attune our perceptions to more than our own experiences, thus opening the possibility—the necessity—of attending to the experiences of others.

Intersectional feminism can be hard; it can be uncomfortable, and it is also utterly vital to the construction of a more just future.

I see now, after more than a decade and after my naïve declaration in that classroom, that while so many gains have been made through feminist work, there is still so much work to do. Much of that is the emotional labour of listening and learning. Of beginning to understand how patriarchal culture sediments inside of us—as well as on us—in our daily lives. Of starting to recognize that patriarchal culture acts on each of us in slightly or radically different ways, but that one person's lived reality is as important and vital as another's. We each move through the world in our own skin, in our own realities. Sometimes, if we're lucky, those realities have commonalities. Other times, if we're equally lucky, those realities are drastically different, and we can learn from one another and practice our capacity for empathy. But too often we see from the myopia of our own experience; we feel that ours is the hardest path, or "theirs" is not "our" problem. How wrong. How narrow. How cowardly. But also, how normal, or at least, how normalized.

*

So where do we begin?

I'm thinking of the question students that have asked me and the question that I ask myself: Where do we begin, when the work of deconstructing, dismantling, and burning down oppressive systems seems so immense?

First, we situate ourselves. Then, we widen the scope of our looking. Then, we situate ourselves again. And repeat.

*

Look back again at the answers you came up with. Several of the questions ask you to think about how you feel in relation to the expectations of others. Namely, they ask you to think about how your way of being in the world has either chafed against the expectations of others or made you feel uncomfortable. And they ask you to think about what it's like for your way of being *not* to chafe against others, but for that compromise to make you feel stifled.

The complex ways in which our personal feelings are mediated by our experiences in the world and by the social structures and expectations of the world in which we live can be summed up in a single term: affect. Scholars of affect pay close attention to feelings that appear to be subjective (our own) but, upon closer study, can be understood to have social, political, and cultural roots and forms of circulation. Affects are private feelings, which, through their circulation in publics, have been rendered political and social.

In other words, "affect" is an umbrella term for acknowledging that as individuals in the world, we encounter forces of feeling that have material effects on our bodies and beings. Sound abstract? It is, but consider this: Have you been in a room full of people when the climate has suddenly and fundamentally changed? Perhaps because of something that was said or because someone entered or left the room. That barometrical shift is affect at work. The cold sweat? The raised pulse? The hairs on your arms standing up as a result of a feeling? That is affect marking your body's *belonging to a world of encounters*.[16] Affect is a combination of external public events and individual and collective responses to them. For our purposes, I'll be focusing on the ways in which affects are read onto gendered bodies and, in turn,

---

16. Melissa Gregg and Gregory J. Seigworth define affect this way in their introduction to *The Affect Theory Reader* (Durham: Duke UP, 2010) 2.

how we internalize and perform those affects—sometimes consciously and sometimes not.

★

Julia Kristeva has written about how women's bodies have been culturally constructed to launder the negative affects of others.[17] I think about this often when actually doing the laundry.

★

Ahmed, an affect scholar, brilliantly theorizes the intersections between gender, race, sexuality, and culture. In other words, she is an intersectional feminist scholar. Moreover, she is an intersectional feminist scholar who—wonder of wonders!—does her thinking in public. This is a generous move and a rare one. Scholars aren't really known for airing drafts of thinking in public. Or, if you are privy to the academic world, that draft-airing more often than not comes in the form of the conference paper that starts with the caveat *this comes from a larger project...* and there goes the next forty-five minutes of your life. I digress. Or do I? Those over-long papers delivered by one academic for a room of other academics are their own form of privileged space-taking, aren't they?

---

17. Julia Kristeva, *Strangers to Ourselves*, trans. Leon S. Roudiez (New York: Columbia UP, 1991) 53.

Anyway, back to Ahmed.

In August of 2013, Ahmed launched her blog *feministkilljoys* as a public companion piece to the more private process of writing her new book, *Living a Feminist Life*. She briefly describes the dual project as *taking off from experiences of being a feminist killjoy at the family table, as well as an angry woman of colour at feminist tables or an angry queer of colour at queer tables. We learn so much from what we come up against!*[18]

The chafing against things such as others' notions of "happiness," then, is useful. It can teach us something about ourselves and what Ahmed refers to as our *relatings* in this world. Let's start keeping track of the chafing. Seriously.

One place to start is with the term "feminist killjoy." When I told my mother that I was thinking of writing a handbook about how to be a feminist killjoy, she expressed concern. Why did I want to make things harder for myself? Aren't there enough epithets about willful subjects circulating without me deliberately taking one up for myself? Well, yes and no. The term "killjoy" tends to be derisive: someone who is a wet blanket, who rains on the parade. The person who says "quiet down" to people engaged in riotous laughter. But when appended to the term "feminist," "killjoy" acquires nuance. "Feminist" is too often understood as inherently and problematically militant. When brought

---

18. Sara Ahmed, "Hello feminist killjoys!" *feministkilljoys* 26 Aug 2013 <www.feministkilljoys.com/2013/08/26/hello-feminist-killjoys/>.

43

together, "feminist" and "killjoy" trouble the habitual understandings of each other. Double positives? Not quite, but taken together they usefully disrupt expectations and so-called common sense.

*

The feminist killjoy takes pleasure in the work of interrupting the patriarchal norms that pass as joys.

*

Burn it down! She gleefully lights the match.

*

According to Ahmed, a feminist killjoy is someone whose existence "makes sense" when we situate her within the context of an intersectional feminist critique of happiness. What do we mean by happiness, really? Much has been written about the pursuit of happiness in both scholarly and popular realms, and the only common denominator is that these days happiness is as much a socialized and commodified product as it is a subjective and individual experience of lightness. Happiness is elusive *and* it is a social imperative. Capitalism suggests we can buy happiness; liberalism posits happiness as an integral part of citizenship (at least in North America); and neoliberalism implies that happiness is hyper-mobile and hyper-accessible if only we buy into it.

But what if we are neither happy in the conventional sense, nor are we quite certain that we agree with the social and subjective imperatives that conventional happiness implies? What if happiness *chafes us*?

For Ahmed, that discomfort tells us something important. Being happy puts us in line with dominant belief systems, such as patriarchy, capitalism, neoliberalism, racism. Being happy, for Ahmed, means we "line up" with what is expected of us. But so much of contemporary life rubs against this so-called happiness. If you're a woman, a queer person, a trans person, a person of colour, or a poor person—in other words, if you're a person who does not fit neatly into the narrow definitions of white, straight, economically-stable masculinity—it is more than likely that your experiences do not readily line up with what you're told should make you happy. That feeling of not-quite-lining up, of not-quite-fitting, can be isolating, alienating, and disempowering. Our attempts to line up with the dominant conception of happiness can also keep those systems that are fuelled by the happiness imperative in fine working order. This self-harming pursuit of impossible happiness is another form of Berlant's notion of cruel optimism.

Happiness as restricted access. Happiness as a country club, a resort, an old boy's club for certain boys only. Happiness as body-shame, as racism, as transphobia, as misogyny. These are some of the joys that need killing.

*

Enter the feminist killjoy.

*

She is a positive figure, the killjoy, though it may take some unlearning to see her as such. The feminist killjoy is not okay with the status quo. She is not settled in the social narratives that are prescribed for her. She will not be conscripted or coerced into restrictive categories of gender or gender performance. She will not tolerate casual instances of racism or classism. She won't keep quiet to maintain a smooth dinner conversation. Oh, no. The feminist killjoy is one who understands that to be a world-maker and to make space for herself in the world, she must disrupt the complacency that the happiness imperative demands. In response to critiques that she's calling out the happiness imperative and rattling the bars of the status quo, the feminist killjoy affirms, "Yes!"

*

Then she rattles some more.

Chapter 1:
Notes on Rape Culture

Girlhood, a brief history of everyday violence
(after Anne Thériault)[1]

I am not sure how old I am. My great aunt slaps my legs and tells me not to sit like that. Good girls don't sit with their legs open.

*

I am in fourth grade. I walk home followed by two boys from my class yelling at me about my breasts. I don't yet wear a bra.

---

1. Anne Thériault wrote "Being a Girl: A Brief Personal History of Violence" on Belle Jar (<http://bellejar.ca/2015/12/03/being-a-girl-a-brief-personal-history-of-violence/>). It blew my mind and legitimized the violences in my own life as experiences worth naming, and trying to name.

*

I am in fifth grade. At camp I share a cabin with a friend of Kristen French. We talk about being afraid to walk home alone. I am in fifth grade. Walking to school with a friend. A man walks by with his penis out, masturbating. We don't have this language, obviously. We giggle nervously. Tell no one. I am in fifth grade. Children are getting snatched. The ubiquitous white van of childhood. Free kittens and candy and all that. At the park, where I am allowed to go alone, I see a man under the jungle gym. Masturbating while we play above him (*Vito Acconci redux?*[2] I think now, ruefully. Angrily.)

*

I am in sixth grade. I am told by a classmate that I am obviously a slut because when I stand straight my knees don't touch. I work to make them touch.

*

I am in ninth grade. I run through the woods to escape a man who is trying to force me into his car.

---

2. Vito Acconci's piece *Seedbed* was first performed in 1972 at the Sonnabend Gallery in New York. The piece involved Acconci lying under a wooden walkway in the gallery, masturbating, while his spoken desires about viewers walking overhead were projected on a loudspeaker in the gallery.

*

I am in high school; I get my driver's license. My mother gives me pepper spray for the glove compartment. I am grateful, think nothing much of it, put it in my glove compartment. Not once do I think, "Why should I carry pepper spray?" I just know it's wise.

*

Still, I am in high school, still. It is interminable, high school. At a party one of my classmates, who is drunk, gets aggressive and insistent that I make out with him. I laugh, try to keep him laughing, as I fall over furniture trying to get away from him. He pushes me. I fall down. Just then, another friend comes into the room.

*

There's more. I don't talk about it much.

*

I am in university. I am living in British Columbia. I am living in Quebec. I go to Europe, alone. I am living in Alberta. I am living in Nova Scotia. I am living in New Brunswick. I am a student. I am a café worker. I am unemployed. I am travelling. I am a graduate student. I am a wife. I am divorced. I am a professor. I am a mom. I am a partner. I am a daughter. I am my own person. I have a history of sexual assault that

I don't talk about. I am careful. I regulate my movement. I worry. I fret. I get fucking angry at having to pay for a cab rather than walk. I walk and am scared. I am in my office and am scared. I am alone at a gas station, late, filling up the truck, scared. I lock the doors. I don't wear my earphones at night when I am walking. I regulate my movement. Now and then I still have nightmares. I regulate my movement.

*

Am I teaching my baby to regulate her movement? Is the world already teaching her that?

*

Notes on Rape Culture

I have a thin scar on the top of my right foot. It isn't particularly eye-catching. In fact, I usually can't see it until the summer months, when my winter-white feet have been in the sun for a bit, and the bumps and nicks of my life are more visible on my skin. It isn't the kind of scar that you'd ask someone about. I have several like it.

I got this particular scar when I was running through the woods wearing Birkenstocks. Don't judge me, it was the '90s. Actually, who am I kidding, I still have Birkenstocks. Anyway, I was running through the woods in my sandals because this man had just tried to get me into his car. This was in rural North Carolina. It was midday. The man in the car—I want to say it was a Camaro, but that might just be a whim, the bitchin' Camaro—had pulled up alongside me while I was walking.

It isn't so common, people walking along the Drewery-Virginia Line Road, so I wasn't immediately put on edge by him stopping. He asked if I wanted a ride. I said *no, thanks.* He said *why not, are you too good for me?* And I said *I'm happy walking, that's all.* He said *come on, girl, I'm going to give you a ride.* I said, *no, you're not.* He said *I'm going to make you get in this car.* I said *fuck you* and took off running through kudzu and pine needles and into the woods. I was between my house (empty, my parents still in Canada working) and my neighbours' (retired, wonderful, letting me stay with them so I wasn't alone).

⋆

There were only two houses between where I'd come from and where I was going.

It was about a mile and a half.

⋆

I ran parallel to the road; through the trees I could see the maybe-Camaro rolling along the road, parallel to me. Windows down. I could hear the man yelling, but I couldn't hear what he was saying.

After cutting across the tobacco field (okay, soybean, because this was the '90s, like I said, and there were lawsuits in the courts, and the farmers were changing their crops over to something less litigious), I got to the K.'s house. Colonel K. was home, and came right out because I guess I was yelling. In a rush, I told him what had happened, and he went back outside. Maybe with a shotgun, but again, it was a while ago, and I don't remember clearly. I think I may have imagined the shotgun. By this point the adrenaline had subsided a bit, and I was feeling panicky. Scared. Less in fly-to-survive mode and moving toward oh-my-god-what-almost-happened mode. So whether or not there was an actual shotgun when Colonel K. stepped out and stared down the car, which had circled back to drive by the house, it *felt* like someone was there with a weapon protecting me. It felt good and not good.

★

Good because, hey, I'd just run through the woods in my sandals, scared that I was being chased. And here was some-one safe! Colonel K.!

Not good because I was also scared that I was overreacting, that my fear was foolish.

★

So, the scar. It was from some pine twigs that had become jammed under the strap of my sandal as I ran. All I had to show for this, my twenty minutes or so of running parallel to the road that I lived on: a wee little scar on my foot.

We went inside, had lemonade, and never talked about it again. What was there to talk about? Nothing had happened.

*

I kept walking on the road in front of my house. Of course I did. It was the country, I like walking, what are you going to do? But I started walking with the dog. And once, when a car went by and honked at me, without thinking I gave it the finger. Later, my friend called to tell me that he had been in the car, with his grandfather. *Oops*, I said. *Sorry*, I said. *My fault. Please tell your grandfather I'm sorry.*

*

Looking at the scar on my foot makes me angry. I look at it, from time to time, and think, *Is this when I learned to fear rape?* And more specifically, is this when I was taught to fear a particular kind of rape? Is this when the "stranger-danger" mantra of childhood finally made sense? And speaking of sense, is this when the vague but ever-present sensations of being in danger were finally made concrete? Was this the moment in which all my self-surveillance and hyper-awareness were vindicated? Like, aha! I *was* in danger all this time?

*

What makes me angry is that the answer is no. No, I learned about rape—and the system of cultural oppression that makes it possible—some other, earlier time. Not through an individual event, but through an accretion of small and big aggressions working themselves out on my body and my mind. The senses, tones, discourses, and experiences that actively taught me to shape my behaviour and my thinking: these aggressions live in my body. I am a somatic archive. We all are. And the culture we live in—a culture in which women fear for their safety and must protect themselves from sexual violence—begets the oppressive system that has taught me to enact or metabolize concrete *and* abstract acts of devastating violence. Women are surveilled, regulated, and objectified. I know this. I learned it young. We all do. This—this makes me angry.

Emilie Buchwald, among others, has defined this infuriating culture as rape culture. She writes that rape culture is *a complex set of beliefs that encourages male sexual aggression and supports violence against women. It is a society where violence is seen as sexy and sexuality as violent. In a rape culture, women perceive a continuum of threatened violence that ranges from sexual remarks to sexual touching to rape itself. A rape culture condones physical and emotional terrorism against women as the norm... In a rape culture both men and women assume that sexual violence is a fact of life, inevitable... However... much of what we accept as inevitable is in fact the expression of values and attitudes that can change.*[3]

In other words, rape culture is shorthand for the reasons why women are taught to protect themselves from *being* raped, the consequence of which is that men are assumed to always already be potential rapists. Moreover, rape culture encompasses all facets of sexualized violence, which means that it shows up everywhere, from sexualized advertisements to campus hazing rituals to drug kits for testing your drink at the bar. Rape culture normalizes sexualized violence. That normalization is what taught me—so early—simultaneously to fear rape *and* not to make a big deal about that fear, because the forces that catalyze my fear are "natural." Indeed, the effects of rape culture may well have you thinking *but being able to test my drink is a great idea!* rather than thinking *marketing and selling a drug testing kit to women rather than eradicating a culture of date rape drugs is kind of crazy.* I—we—have been taught to both fear rape and know that it's inevitable in some valance. That normalization has created moments of what Rebecca Blakey calls *meta-cognition*: when you know you're being taught something, but you don't have the language yet for what it is you're being taught.

*

3. Emilie Buchwald, Pamela Fletcher, Martha Roth, ed., *Transforming a Rape Culture* (Minneapolis: Milkweed Editions, 1994) xi.

Good girls don't sit like that.

★

Smart girls don't walk alone.

★

I'm sorry that you scared me and that I gave you and your grand-father the finger.

★

I think surely some percentage of women hasn't been raped. I don't know though, really. Perhaps this is the kind of thing I could find out on Google.[4]

I have been trying to remember the first time I heard the word "rape," never mind the term "rape culture." I can't remember, and this seems significant to me. Certainly, I can pinpoint key moments in my childhood when I could feel the charged energy of what I would now name rape culture. I can list moments of warning that taught me to be careful, taught me to be aware, and, I see now, taught me that my own safety was my responsibility. But I can't come up with a key moment when I heard the word *rape*. Not until I was in university. Not until I was in a course on feminist political theory. So, not until I was about twenty.

---

4. Claudia Rankine, *Don't Let Me Be Lonely: An American Lyric* (Minneapolis: Graywolf Press, 2004) 72.

Don't get me wrong, I knew what rape was before I ended up taking the course as one of my electives. But honestly, my understanding of what "counted" as rape was pulled from spectacular and shocking representations of it, the likes of which ended up on television. *Law & Order: SVU.* *CSI.* That sort of stuff. It never occurred to me—or many of my friends—that non-consensual sex, especially with people we knew, could ever be named. Instead, if we talked to each other about it at all, we did it in vague and veiled terms. *It was a bad night. No, I'm not going to see him again. No, I don't want to talk about it, I'm fine. Nothing happened.*

*

Why is it that rape and the spectre of rape—that vague, hazy, ever-present possibility of rape—are so difficult to clearly define? Why is it that every time an assault case makes it into the mainstream media, there is so much time spent speculating about what happened, how it happened, and whether it was, actually, an indefensible instance of sexual assault or rape? Or worse, that there is so much time spent framing the assault as benign, an unfortunate misunderstanding, an overreaction on the part of the hysterical accuser. Why is it that so much time and energy is spent denying the validity of someone who says: *I have been assaulted. I have been raped. I have been hurt. Something has happened. Someone did this to me.* I think a space opens to deny or deflect accusations because rape is primarily represented as an unmistakable spectacle of violence when, in fact, rape encompasses a devastatingly wide array of public and private violences. We learn quickly that, like a spectre, the possibility of rape is everywhere at once. We are taught that, like a spectre, rape is almost impossible to pin down.

*

Do you remember that Stephen King novel *It*? That's the novel with the terrifying clown-killer. In the novel, *It* hunts its prey, who are children, by taking the form of their deepest fears. I hate horror as a genre. I appreciate the ways in which scholars have demonstrated that horror reflects deeply contemporary anxieties and pathologies, but me? I get nightmares. Still, I'm struck by the prescience of *It*, by the incredibly succinct way that King gives form to the haziness of fears we learn before we have words for them. Rape and its spectre are both an *It*.

*

In my feminist theory class in undergrad at UNC, we read what I have now come to think of as some of the canonical feminist texts: Marilyn Frye's *The Politics of Reality*, Patricia Hill Collins's *Black Feminist Thought,* Gloria Anzaldúa and Cherríe Moraga's anthology *This Bridge Called My Back,* Catherine MacKinnon's *Toward A Feminist Theory of the State*. I struggled with all of these books, for different reasons. New language, new paradigms of thought, knowledge written on bodies that were differently raced and sexed than mine.

The readings in this course, which clearly situate me as a university student of the late 1990s, were the first places I started to grasp the kind of language and thinking I needed to understand the world in which I, in my gendered body, was living. It was here, I think, that I started to develop a language with which to articulate what my body had internalized already.

The French language makes linguistic room for different ways of knowing. *Connaître* means to know viscerally, while *savoir* is to know factually. It was in this classroom, listening to other, more politicized students, that I started to find words to give shape to the hazy *it* of knowledge. I became savvy (linked to *savoir?*), I suppose. I found words for what my body already knew. Though at times what my body knew stood in opposition to what appeared as "fact." It was poetry that taught me that paradox was real and valuable. Poetry taught me that paradox was also a form of knowledge.

*

Here's the thing: we don't know how to talk about rape. We don't know how to differentiate between different experiences of rape. We don't know how to address the perniciousness of rape in history as a calculated tool for violence and subordination any more than we know how to discuss rape as a sometimes-facet of otherwise consensual sexual relationships.

Without clear terms and clear lines that define rape, assault, and rape culture, we wind up with a climate of public discussion that, as its means of addressing violence, almost-always veers to blaming the person who has endured rape.

In Canada, sexual harm and rape are defined in a series of specific provisions in the Criminal Code of Canada. The laws and provisions themselves are extremely specific about what does and does not constitute consent, but the application of those laws is troubled because it emerges from entrenched gendered assumptions about sex and sexuality. In short, a society's assumptions about gender, sex, sexuality, and sexual violence *profoundly* affect how laws are interpreted and applied by juries and judges alike.

It occurs to me that a task of the feminist killjoy is killing the slippery, hazy vagaries that surround discussions of both rape and rape culture. The killjoy's job is to interrupt the habitual flows of patriarchal discourse, of rape and rape culture. This act of interruption—of interruption as articulation—brings the spectre of gender-based and sexualized violence into focus, makes it harder to deny or justify. Naming that violence, articulating the conditions of its existence, and working to alter those conditions is the work of killing this so-called joy.

*

I think the figures of the strange and the stranger have something to offer in this work.

I mean, think about it: Rape is sensationalized as an act of violence perpetuated in spectacularly violent ways by a strange man against a vulnerable woman. The rapist is always figured as a stranger, though we know that a large percentage of rape and sexualized violence is done by people we know. By an early age I had learned to fear the man following me in his car; but no one taught me that I might have to fear people I knew.

A large part of the supposed 20% [of people who have been raped] is that you have to know what rape means to even say you were raped. I was recently talking about this encounter with my therapist and how deeply the perpetuated myth of the rapist goes. The mace on your keychain given to you by your mother won't help in the bedroom of someone you know, trust, or potentially love.[5]

Horrific acts of violence are done by strangers to strangers, but pathologizing a rapist primarily as a singular *monster just beyond the margins of culture* is not only inaccurate; it is *also* a narrative that sustains rape culture. The rendering of rapists as alien "others," as strangers, in turn renders rape "other" and inhuman. Situating the rapist outside of the culture that he supposedly violates, the rapist remains an anomaly rather than a product of patriarchal culture.

For a concrete example of what I mean, think back to the structure of shows like *Law & Order: SVU*. These shows

---

5. Cassandra Troyan, "The Body Always Remembers: An Interview with Amy Berkowitz," *The New Inquiry* 24 Sept 2015 <http://thenewinquiry. com/features/the-body-always-remembers/>.

are based on reckoning with rape, but it's a strange kind of reckoning. Here, more often than not, the violence is framed as an encounter with a monster, not a neighbour. The structure of *SVU*, for example, moves from a violent event to the hunt for the monster, from working with the victim to the monster's day in court. The moral arc of the show tends to reinforce the otherness of violence without asking us to consider the systems in which the violence is fostered. The rapist is always a sadist and not "normal." What gets punished, then, is the difference that the rapist manifests—his strangeness, his sadism—rather than the rape itself.

We cannot afford to let rape remain alien, other, or strange, because clearly that narrative doesn't work. It doesn't stop anyone from raping. Rather, it offers an alibi to the more common occurrence of rape by friend or acquaintance (or a loved one or a family member or new dating interest or co-worker or boss) and to the quotidian nature of violence against women and the cultural structures that foster that violence.

Talking about violence against women (and not rape in particular), Nicole Brossard is unequivocally clear on this point. In her incisive essay, "The Killer Was No Young Man," published shortly after the 1989 Polytechnique Massacre in Montreal, Brossard refutes the media's narrative of the killer as a "lone wolf," which makes him a stranger, different from other humans, singular. The media emblematized the murdered women as victims of an *enraged gunman*, thus allowing the public to disregard the fact that the gunman's act was predicated on a historical and legal legacy of viewing women as non-subjects. *All things considered*, says Brossard, *M.L. was no young man. He was as old as all the sexist, misogynist proverbs, as old as all the Church fathers who doubted women had a soul. He was as old as all the legislators who ever forbade women the university, the right to vote, access to the public sphere. M.L. was as old as Man and his contempt for women.*[6]

Brossard asserts that the killer's actions, though denounced as uniquely reprehensible, were enactments of the same violences that have been performed for centuries and are still being performed now in rhetoric and in daily life. And notice Brossard's sleight of hand: Rather than articulate his proper name, she refuses M.L. the power of direct reference.[7] Her refusal to name the killer underscores her larger refusal to perpetuate linguistic violence, which is inseparable, as she states, from physical violence. By refusing M.L. the spotlight of the proper name, Brossard refuses him the infamy of his violent acts. This isn't about M.L., alone, with his anger and his gun. This is about the history of misogyny. At the same time, Brossard doesn't anonymize M.L. to the point

6. Nicole Brossard, "The Killer Was No Young Man," *The Montreal Massacre*, ed. Louise Malette and Marie Chalouh. Trans. Marlene Wildeman (Charlottetown: gynergy, 1991) 31–33.

7. Anderson Cooper enacts this same kind of refusal when he reads the names and ages of the forty-nine people massacred at Pulse and explains his refusal to give space to or say the name of their murderer. See <http://news.nationalpost.com/news/world/anderson-cooper-breaks-down-while-reading-names-of-orlando-shooting-victims>.

of unrecognizability. Rather, she uses his initials, appending his actions to him, and she contextualizes him and his reprehensible violence in the long history of patriarchal culture. Brossard unmasks M.L.'s strangeness, situating his actions within a history of patriarchal violence. By refusing to situate him with his proper name *and* refusing to make him a stranger, Brossard forges a middle ground from which M.L. emerges as part of a lineage. He is a figure bound to and borne of a history of violence. In so doing, she removes the haze from the horror.

★

Sara Ahmed also writes of the dangers posed by the figure of the stranger. For her, the figure is both fetish and fear embodied. Fascinating and fearful, the stranger lurks at the limits of my knowing. And that liminality—for the one cast as strange and for me, taught to fear strangeness and strangers—is damaging for everyone.

In *Strange Encounters,* Ahmed unpacks the ways in which strangers circulate as cultural commodities and tools of fear. She borrows from Marx's explanation of commodity fetishism to propose another kind of fetishism: a *fetishism of figures*. In Marx's explanation, commodities gain both stature and financial value not through their inherent worth but through their fetish status. Ahmed dislocates fetishism from the commodity and affixes it to the way that ideas about character types—figures—get fetishized. In other words, she suggests that a general sense of character types—the mom, the bro, the stranger—sediments in our minds through fetishistic function. Her analysis focuses on the figure of the stranger, and she posits that *the stranger can appear as a figure, one we assume has a life of its own, by being cut off from the history of its determination. To write about this figure is to give it a history; but of course, it is always possible that in following a figure one can retain it as a fetish, as if the qualities it has acquired can be contained by its form.*[8] Picture a silhouette, maybe one of those profile paper cuttings done in black of a Victorian child. Indistinct, faceless, the silhouette could be almost anyone. Now flesh it out and make that silhouette whole; put a body on it. We can recognize the form—a person—but the form is still anonymous. Embodiment allows the stranger to move through the world, but the shadows remain; the stranger is never wholly knowable. That, I think, is what Ahmed is getting at: the stranger becomes a figure, a conjurable being whom we can imagine and to which we can give form, but one whose specific identity is always unknown. Rather than casting a light on the stranger, we find it easier, more manageable, to leave him strange.

If the only narratives about rape that we have in mainstream culture are of random acts of violence undertaken by a monster, then how can we ever hope to give the space and respect and language needed to speak to the myriad of experiences that are outside of this myopic account? What

---

8. Sara Ahmed, "In the Company of Strangers," *feministkilljoys* 10 Nov 2013 <http://feministkilljoys.com/2013/11/10/in-the-company-of-strangers/>. Ahmed's book interrogates the history of inherent racialization and racism associated with the figure of the stranger.

if we articulated the haziness around definitions and articulations of rape and rape culture—the spectre of rape—as a making strange of rape? Maintaining the stranger or the monster or the lone wolf as a figure for rapists saves us from having to cast light on who rapes whom. Without specificity, we don't have to look at loved ones, family, friends, or colleagues. We may not have to look at ourselves. The rapist remains strange and a stranger.

Instead, borrowing the language of Publius Terentius Afer, it would be more productive to say: *I am human, and nothing of that which is human is alien to me.*[9]

*

When we begin to understand our public discourse around rape as a narrative of making strange, we can begin to see how women's experiences of rape and rape culture work to make them strangers *to themselves*. The body knows. My body knows. But the ways in which we talk about rape

---

9. Publius Terentius Afer (a.k.a., just plain old "Terence") said that. While he was enslaved, Terence was educated by a Roman senator who eventually freed him. Terence became a playwright and wrote six plays before his death. All of the plays survive to this day. I am not an expert in the history of Roman slaveholding, but it seems to me that one tactic that societies participating in slave economies use to justify their acts of violence against other humans is to represent those enslaved humans as less-than human. With this in mind, Terence's statement becomes even more radically open. He claims his humanity and the humanity of others, and his words don't make room for an escape from our own acts. There's no place for making strange and making strangers. There are just people doing things to other people.

sound like this: *Your experiences? No. They don't count. You're just paranoid / overly sensitive / you misunderstood what happened / you're wrong.* Or: *You were asking for it / you shouldn't have been there, alone, walking / you were wrong.*

*

Every now and then in the writing of this, I catch myself holding my breath or staring at the computer screen while I *actually* wring my hands. Or I feel my heart racing. Or I am sharp. I want to yell, but I don't know whom to yell at. And that's usually where the physical affects of my anger shift to something else. Exhaustion. Despair. I cry while I'm writing, and this, too, pisses me off. It makes my nose run. It makes me feel weak, even though I know I am not. I know that crying is not a sign of weakness. Will anyone read this? And, if they read it, will they use it against me? I am already anticipating the hate mail.

Each time I experience these physical reminders of the anger and outrage that I carry with me on a daily basis, I am returned to the ways in which they—these feelings—are also part of rape culture. I remember that they need to be addressed and worked through. It is *work*. And that work makes me tired and angry.

*

So before anything else, let me pause here. Let me stay with how a feminist killjoy might deal with her anger. Let me think about whether anger can *do* anything, and if we can do anything with anger.

*

Who gets to be angry?

At least since Freud pathologized women's anger—and any other "excessive" display of emotion—as evidence of hysteria, anger has fallen under the umbrella of too-muchness. And this devaluation and depoliticization of women's emotions only *increases* if you are a woman of colour; especially, as Blair L. M. Kelley writes, if you are a Black woman. *The first "black women" American audiences saw on the American stage were minstrel "Negro wenches," writes Kelly. Using burned cork and greasepaint to blacken their skin, white men performed as black men and women; these performances became wildly popular in the mid-19th century. White men used crude drag along with the burned cork to mark black women as grotesque, loud-mouthed, masculine and undeserving of the protections afforded to white "ladies" in American society.*[10] In other words, white male minstrel performers enacted the first so-called popular representations of Black women, and they did so in public performances that used racism and ridicule in the service of "humour." In these shows, Black women's anger was not their own; their anger was a derogatory performance

10. Blair L.M. Kelley, "Here's Some History Behind that 'Angry Black Woman' Riff the *New York Times* Tossed Around." The Root 25 Sept 2014 <http://www.theroot.com/articles/culture/2014/09/the_angry_black_woman_stereotype_s_long_history.html>.

68

enacted by white men. And yet the restrictive and racist trope of the "Angry Black Woman," which does not emerge out of Black women's own forms of anger but rather out of racist representations of it, sticks to this day. White audiences loved that disrespectful shit—still do, I fear—and that is an example of patriarchal joy that needs killing.

*

Who gets to be angry?

*

Sianne Ngai has written about the ways in which white patriarchal culture dilutes strong affective experiences, especially when they are experienced by racialized women. For example, rather than write about anger, Ngai writes about an affect she calls *animatedness*. Animatedness, for Ngai, is the byproduct of the racialization of emotion. It occurs when people of colour are characterized as effusively emotional—"zesty" and "lively" are but two examples of this thinly veiled subjugation of emotion. As Eu Jin Chua writes, *excessive emotionality [in Ngai's work] becomes the paradoxical index of a very real subjugation, the sign of a racial logic in which rational (emotionless) autonomy is ascribed only to white male subjects.*[11]

---

11. Eu Jin Chua, "Review of Sianne Ngai's Ugly Feelings," *Bryn Mawr Review of Comparative Literature* 6 (2/2007) <http://www.brynmawr.edu/bmrcl/Ugly%20Feelings.htm>.

Here's the thing: even emotion is susceptible to the repressive mechanisms of patriarchal culture. We can feel all the feelings, but there is absolutely no guarantee our feelings will be read as legitimate. Anger, when expressed by white women, women of colour, people of colour, differently abled people, queer people, and trans-people, gets repackaged and represented as something else, something less powerful: animatedness, hysteria, otherness.

Patriarchy, as my dear friend and colleague R. wrote to me, is a joy (in the unironic sense of the word) that women and other Others do not experience. *But* as a white woman, white supremacy is a joy I do experience. I experience the "joys" of white supremacy and white privilege in the way that men experience the "joys" of patriarchy—in a state of blissful unconsciousness. What R. means is that I benefit from this "joy" that needs killing, so I'm not forced to do the daily hard work of thinking through it, chafing against it, and resisting its attempts to delegitimize my life. What R. means is that it's easy for me and other white women *not* to do the work. What she means is that even though patriarchal culture chafes me and wounds me, my whiteness gives me more privilege than others have in this unequal system. So one of my responsibilities, as a white, cis-gendered woman, is to learn how to be a traitor to the "joys" of patriarchal culture that I experience, however unconsciously. As R. puts it, *we have to learn how we become weaponized against certain bodies. And then we need to learn to re-weaponize against the systems, not the bodies.* Learn how you experience certain "joys" that afford you comfort zones that others don't get.

Learn how to stop participating in your unearned privilege. Kill that joy and fight with other Others in solidarity.

*

A feminist call might be a call to anger, to develop a sense of rage about collective wrongs. And yet, it is important that we do not make feminist emotion into a site of truth: as if it is always clear or self-evident that our anger is right.[12]

That's Sara Ahmed writing about the feminist killjoy and other willful subjects. Ahmed draws on Black feminist writing generally, and Audre Lorde specifically, to think through the ways in which anger is crucial for the necessary energy to react against injustice. Lorde writes:

My fear of anger taught me nothing.... Anger expressed and translated into action in the service of our vision and our future is a liberating and strengthening act of clarification.... Anger is loaded with information and energy.[13]

Anger, as Ahmed puts it, is framed here as a *response to injustice; as a vision and version of the future; as a translation of pain into knowledge.* Anger, she writes, is not simply a response

---

12. All of the Ahmed quotations on anger in this section come from "Feminist Killjoys (And Other Willful Subjects)." *Polyphonic Feminisms: Acting in Concert*, ed. Mandy Van Deven and Julia Kubala. *The Scholar & Feminist Online* <http://sfonline.barnard.edu/polyphonic/ahmed_04.htm>.

13. Audre Lorde, *Sister Outsider: Essays and Speeches* (Berkeley, CA: Crossing Press, 2007) 124, 127.

to the past; it is also an opening up into the future. It is a means of moving forward out of what is without forgetting what was. *If anger energizes feminist subjects, it also requires those subject to "read" and "move" from anger into a different bodily world.*

Ahmed and Lorde are not the only writers who extol the vitality of anger for a feminist, anti-racist, social justice movement, but they are two that I find myself coming back to again and again because they articulate so clearly for me why anger is necessary and empowering.

And why anger is only a beginning. Here is Ahmed again:

When anger becomes righteous it can be oppressive; to assume anger makes us right can be a wrong…. Emotions are not always just, even those that seem to acquire their force in or from an experience of injustice. Feminist emotions are mediated and opaque; they are sites of struggle, and we must persist in struggling with them.[14]

This gets me every time I read it: *When anger becomes righteous it can be oppressive.*

Oof. I mean, part of what I appreciate about righteous anger is, well, how right it makes me feel. Justified. Indisputable in my emotional response.

---

14. Ahmed.

*

I have been guilty of this oppressive righteousness, I think. When I was unfairly passed over for a permanent job I had worked really hard for and was more than qualified to do, I became righteously angry. After I peeled myself off the floor (okay, my partner helped peel me off the floor over the course of several months), I couldn't stop the anger from flooding out of my mouth. I seethed. Anger seeped out of me. I felt *good*, because this wrong was a wrong that others recognized as such. No equivocation; what had happened was *wrong*. But after a while, after months of radiating an anger that moved me through my day, after vibrating with an anger so incandescent that listening to myself talk was like an out-of-body experience, my righteous anger didn't sustain me. And then it just made me tired. And now, though the situation hasn't changed, though that wrong hasn't been publicly acknowledged or righted, though I still don't have steady employment in the field I've worked in for more than a decade, and though my anger hasn't dissipated, my righteousness has burned out.

*

Why?

*

I think, upon reflection, that it has to do with what Ahmed warns the feminist killjoy about. It's not that anger isn't useful or even necessary for feminist killjoys. In fact, in *The Cultural Politics of Emotion*, Ahmed writes about the necessity of anger for the feminist movement. Rather, what I read in her words is a caution: Don't let your anger—especially if it is righteous, especially if you *know* you're on the side of right—fool you into thinking that it makes *you* right. Don't be precious about your anger, warns Ahmed. Don't let your anger become a site of oppression—for you, for others—when it can be a site of struggle. Don't let your own experience of anger—feminist, justified, understandable—become totemic. Don't let your anger be a stopping point. Don't let your anger stop you from doing the hard feminist work of killing the joys of patriarchal culture. Don't let your anger blind you to the anger others experience, differently. Don't think your anger is universal. Don't think because your anger is feminist that it is meaningful for all women. Don't fetishize your anger.

*

Going back to Ahmed's quote again: *Feminist emotions are mediated and opaque.* So how does the feminist killjoy manage anger as a reasonable response to rape culture? Can anger motivate movement rather than keep us cycling through a feedback loop of volcanic emotion? How might we *persist in struggling* with anger?

*

Killing the "joys" of patriarchal culture means training

ourselves to recognize these systemic oppressions and also organizing against them.

When positioned externally, as a site of struggle, rather than locked inside me as a self-referential feedback loop, anger can provide traction:

If anger is a form of "against-ness," then it is precisely about the impossibility of moving beyond the history of injuries to a pure or innocent position. Anger does not necessarily require an investment in revenge, which is one form of reaction to what one is against. Being against something is dependent on how one reads what one is against.... The question becomes: What form of action is possible given that reading?

Anger isn't just about that old wound that happened in the past. Instead, as Ahmed writes, anger can be a way of moving into the future that remembers the wrong but isn't stuck there with no way forward.

★

I am trying to think differently about that scar on my foot now. When I look at it, that pale trace of an event, I am still angry. But I am trying to use the anger that I feel—about this and other events—as a text to be read and revised, read and revised. I am trying to position my anger as a form of *against-ness* for myself and for encountering and working with others. Certainly, that is what this chapter is: positioning my anger at rape and rape culture as a form of *against-ness.* Against explaining it away. Against reductive narratives. Against victim-blaming. Against internalization and towards another form of public discussion.

*

Back, then, to one of those so-called joys that the feminist killjoy is working against. Back to thinking through one of those so-called joys that bring us to places of anger, to places of risky self-righteousness.

Back, once more, to the pervasive "joy" of rape culture. It is a strange thing to call rape culture a joy, isn't it? Strange, too, to call rape a culture. And yet, here we are. As Ahmed suggests, the so-called joys of patriarchal culture don't just chafe against feminist killjoys and other willful subjects; they actively work to annihilate them.

*

I have spent my whole adult working life on university and college campuses. Really, I became an adult on campus. With the exception of one year (ruefully referred to as "the lost year") spent in a converted 1970s Ford school bus, I have been on university and college campuses every year since 1997, when I started my undergraduate work at the University of North Carolina. I have gone from being a naïve first-year student living in a dormitory to a graduate student newly trying to figure out systems of power to a teaching assistant, research assistant, instructor, and finally, a fully-PhD-ed precarious worker teaching several classes a semester. Campus cultures have become familiar to me. I learned something of who I was and who I was becoming while in university. As cliché as it is to say, I learned something of the world, there in Chapel Hill, in Montreal, in Calgary, surrounded by the ostentatiously gorgeous azaleas and the pervasive smell of wisteria, then the mountain, and then the mountains in the distance.

One of the world-building things I learned was that periodically a tacit understanding between women who are strangers emerges. Like when I started my first university job, working at a café on Franklin Street. Franklin St. is the main drag of Chapel Hill, a classic American university town. The street is wide, tree-lined, and filled with cafés, shops, restaurants, and bars. The university campus bumps right up against the south side of the street: expansive, tree-covered quads peppered with old, ivy-and-wisteria-covered buildings. It is a beautiful campus. The café where I worked was right across from the North Quad. In the fall, we'd watch hundreds of girls who'd pledged sororities run screaming across the grass to their new sorority houses. For me, a transplanted Canadian, it was a bizarre and disconcerting sight. It seemed an exuberant but edgy adaptation of the end of Lars von Trier's *Antichrist* where women ooze out of the woods; only in this version, the women are loud and happy and wearing pastel colours.

Anyway, the café was open until midnight, and I was a dishwasher, so I didn't finish until nearly one in the morning.

Sure, there were Point-to-Point vans (that's what the safe passage on campus transport was called), but they didn't come to the end of town I worked in, and they took forever to get to my dorm on the far edge of campus. Yes, there were cabs, but I was a student working to save money. So I walked. I like walking.

One night, as I started the forty-minute walk home across the tree-filled campus, taking care to avoid the botanical gardens, trying to stay on the lit paths, I became aware of someone else walking. I could see out of the corner of my eye that it was another woman. We matched pace with one another, exchanged one quick glance. That was it. The other woman, whom I recognized from another café, was wearing headphones. We walked a few metres apart. Across the North Quad. Past the Old Well. Across the South Quad. Through the Pit. Down the hill and under the bridge and past the football stadium and the tennis courts all the way to the Hinton James dormitory. We parted ways there. I don't even think we waved. But for that long, quiet walk home in the dark, we didn't lose one another. That's one of the things that I learned on campus: as a woman I was both responsible and culpable for my own physical safety.

Oh, joy.

*

Here is the key point to remember: the so-called "joys" that the feminist killjoy works against are the "joys" of patriarchy. In other words, the feminist killjoy works against things that actually contain no joy for the functionally sane.

Here's another example of "joy" pulled from cultural history's recent archives that also took place on a campus.

In the fall of 2014, an art student at Columbia University by the name of Emma Sulkowicz began carrying her mattress to class. It was a single mattress, the kind issued to a standard dorm room. Picture it: grey with off-white piping and dark pin stripes. Thin. Narrow. Frustratingly awkward to carry in that it is both heavier and more floppy that it looks.

So Emma Sulkowicz starts carrying her mattress on campus; everywhere she goes—to class, to lunch, to study—there it is in her arms: an awkward, protesting companion.

This act of endurance performance, entitled *Carry That Weight*, was her senior thesis project for her Fine Arts Degree.[15] It was also a public acknowledgement of her experience of sexual assault on campus. Sulkowicz was sexually assaulted in her dorm room at the beginning of her second

---

15. As Tatiana A. Koroleva suggests, performance that requires some form of exhaustion, such as pain or solitude or collapse [*Subversive Body in Performance Art* (State University of New York at Buffalo, 2008) 29, 44–46]. Paul Allain and Jen Harvie note that performance art which takes place over a long period of time is also endurance performance [*The Routledge Companion to Theatre and Performance* (New York: Routledge, 2014) 221)]. Marina Abromovic's *The Artist Is Present*, which required Abromovic to sit silently for seventy-five hours while making constant eye contact with gallery attendees, is an example of endurance performance.

year of university. Carrying her fifty-pound mattress around campus was a visual and physical statement both of her assault and of the fact that her rapist was still a student at Columbia. He was unpunished, despite several disclosures of assault from Sulkowicz and other women.

Sulkowicz carried the weight of her assault as she moved through the same space as her assailant.

*

Carry That Weight caught international media attention not long after Sulkowicz began the project. On the whole, media response was positive. Sulkowicz's project was cast as a brave one. Further, classmates and concerned Columbia students even began to help her carry her mattress or to carry their own in a form of visual and physical support. It seemed, for a short moment, that the climate of campus rape culture (as a particularly toxic culture) might finally be shifting away from blaming the person who has endured rape[16] towards a conversation that would make room for teaching consent, for articulating the incredibly murky areas between regret and the realization of violation. It didn't last long.

---

16. Endurance. That's how my friend R. talks about people who have been raped. They have endured it. They are enduring the effects of rape. We are enduring the effects of rape culture. I am drawn to this language, for like endurance art or endurance sport, it makes room for the long-term work of living a life; the life of those enduring rape, however, is fundamentally altered by violence. Endurance also, I think, makes room for agency. I have endured. I endure. I will endure. I will have endured. I'm taking up R.'s language here, rather than the more juridical (not to mention, mainstream) ways in which rape casts someone in the position of victim.

Early in 2015, Sulkowicz received an email from Cathy Young, a journalist for the American news website *The Daily Beast*. In her email to Sulkowicz, Young said she was writing an article in which she had quotations from Sulkowicz's rapist, Paul Nungesser. By this point, Sulkowicz was no stranger to media attention around her performance. Indeed, she wasn't unfamiliar with talking about it in general. While, as Sulkowicz has noted in many interviews, she didn't initially report her assault, she did talk about it informally with other women on campus.

Does that last statement catch you up a bit? I mean the part about not initially reporting her assault? Take a minute and think how you're caught up—because you recognize the reticence to report? Or because you can't understand why she wouldn't report being raped?

Rape is one of the most under-reported violences in the world. Further, as the American-based Center for Public Integrity has reported, as many as ninety-five percent of campus rapes go unreported. Ninety-five percent. Unreported.[17] Is that so hard to understand? Lest we forget this way of thinking flattens experiences into a narrative that maintains the patriarchy foisted upon them. Lest we forget that this narrative flattens experiences into a narrative that benefits the continuation of patriarchy rather than the

---

17. Suzanne Ito, "New Report Shows 95% of Campus Rapes Go Unreported," *ACLU* 25 Feb 2010 <https://www.aclu.org/blog/speakeasy/new-report-shows-95-campus-rapes-go-unreported>.

endurance of women. Lest we forget that if you are denied the validity of your own anger, moving through and beyond that anger is difficult, to say the least.

*

What happens when a rape goes unreported, on campus or off? What happens when a story of violence enacted on a body goes unnamed?

*

When Sulkowicz did decide to report the rape to campus authorities, she was required to appear before a disciplinary panel. Not only did she have to explain the details of her assault and the reasons for her reluctance to report it, she also had to go into painful details about how her assault was physically possible.[18] The panel found her rapist not guilty, and he was allowed to remain a student on campus. Without consequences. With impunity. Unpunished.[19]

---

18. Emma Sulkowicz claims that Nungesser anally raped her. "A Survivor's Burden: Columbia Student Carries Mattress on Campus until Alleged Rapist Is Expelled." Democracy Now! 16 Sept 2014 <http://www.democracynow.org/2014/9/16/a_survivors_burden_columbia_student_carries>.

19. Sulkowicz and her supporters at Columbia began wearing red tape in the form of an X on their arms to signify the red tape that a person who has endured rape must go through in order to report at Columbia. The red tape movement spread beyond Columbia to other university campuses. See <http://www.slate.com/blogs/xx_factor/2014/10/30/carry_that_weight_emma_sulkowicz_s_mattress_becomes_a_national_movement.html>.

Yet, for the most part, when news of the project *Carry That Weight* was picked up by the media, the response was, as I said, mostly positive. Until early 2015, when Sulkowicz was contacted by Young.

Normally, I don't respond to people who use my rapist as collateral in order to make them talk to me, said Sulkowizc in an interview with Julie Zellinger.[20] Yet Young persisted. She informed Sulkowicz that she had more than thirty pages of Facebook correspondence between Sulkowicz and Nungesser, which she wanted to verify and intended to reference in her article. *It's an awful feeling where this reporter is digging through my personal life,* Sulkowicz told Zellinger. *At this point I didn't realize that she [Young] is extremely anti-feminist and would do this in order to shame me.*[21] Indeed, Young has written other pieces that, as Sulkowicz puts it, *support[s] the rapists and make the survivors look unreliable.*[22]

Young published her article under the title "Columbia Student: I Didn't Rape Her." In this piece Young presents facts—the delayed report, the fact that Sulkowicz and Nun-

---

20. From Julie Zellinger, "The Treatment of Emma Sulkowicz Proves We Still Have No Idea How to Talk about Rape," *Identities.Mic* 3 Feb 2015 http://mic.com/articles/109446/the-treatment-of-emma-sulkowicz-proves-we-still-have-no-idea-how-to-talk-about-rape

21. Ibid.

22. Cathy Young, "The UVA Story Unravels: Feminist Agitprop and Rape-Hoax Denialism," *Real Clear Politics* 8 Dec 2014 <http://www.realclear-politics.com/articles/2014/12/08/the_uva_story_unravels_feminist_agit-prop_and_rape-hoax_denialism_124891.html>.

gesser were, for a while, friends with benefits. What she does not present is a nuanced consideration of why anyone might not immediately report an assault, why rape by an acquaintance might be so difficult to navigate, and, crucially, what it means to be able to consent. Instead, Young reprints three pages of Facebook conversation between Sulkowicz and Nungesser after the alleged assault. This conversation, which is almost certainly presented to undermine Sulkowicz's project as well as her accusation and testimony, indeed present cordial communication. Here is a brief excerpt:

> On Aug. 29, two days after the alleged rape, Nungesser messaged Sulkowicz on Facebook to say, "Small shindig in our room tonight—bring cool freshmen." Her response:
>
> lol yusss
>
> Also I feel like we need to have some real time where we can talk about life and thingz because we still haven't really had a paul-emma chill sesh since summmmerrrr

Considering context implies thinking about how something is said and thinking about the way different contexts influence the way we interpret a given text, conversation, or statement. So what is the context of this short message?

That Sulkowicz and Nungesser knew each other; that they were familiars.

Look more closely. What is the context of gender-based

84

violence against women? As Audra Williams has said, *women often respond to danger like this: freeze, appease, mend, tend, befriend.*[23] I'll come back to this more fully in a moment, but let's pause here for a second to let Williams's statement sink in.

Women often respond to danger like this: freeze, appease, mend, tend, befriend.

And if we were to think about the context and content of Williams's statement? Then maybe Sulkowicz's texts make more sense.

*

Unless, of course, you have, like I have, responded to danger by freezing, appeasing, mending, tending, and befriending. Then it all makes sense already.

*

Here are some questions that context forces us to consider: What is the wider context of the sexual relations between university students? What did hook-up culture look like on the Columbia University campus in 2014 amongst this

---

23. Audra Williams's full tweet from February 6, 2016, when Jian Ghomeshi was on trial in Canada: "The trial is a good time to remind folks that women often respond to danger like this: freeze, appease, mend, tend, befriend." She tweets from the handle @audrawilliams; I recommend that readers follow her.

group of people? What were the expectations for men and women in this culture at this time? How are young women taught to navigate their sexuality and independence? And how, if given time for reflection, are young women taught to re-examine their own experiences when those experiences are painful, shocking, or violating?

What, really, do we know about sexual assault and rape that happens amongst people who know each other?

Not enough to make a pronouncement of innocence in a newspaper. Not enough to declare Sulkowicz's endurance performance *a campaign against Nungesser*.[24] Not enough to so demonstratively work to slut-shame the woman and cast the rapist as a misunderstood and persecuted youngster. Because it maps so directly onto the ways in which we are taught to doubt women, Young's account *cannot* coexist with the other readings. Young's report undermines the positive readings of Sulkowicz's project. There are two basic cultural narratives at work in rape culture: 1) the lone wolf/ stranger/sadist who rapes the blameless woman, and 2) the at-fault woman who creates a fuss out of misunderstand-ing/manipulating her own experience out of regret or a desire for fame. Young's piece follows this second line. It reshapes the way that the public reads Sulkowicz, reinforc-ing one of the expected narrative arcs of rape in mainstream

---

24. This statement was made to Cathy Young by Nungesser's father. See <http://www.thedailybeast.com/articles/2015/02/03/columbia-student-i-didn-t-rape-her.html>.

media and culture: it's the woman's fault. It's inevitable. She should have seen it coming. And if she saw it coming and didn't get out of the way, then she's to blame. Or, as Young's report salaciously suggests, she planned it. Instead, I'd argue, Young's report reshapes the way that the public reads Sulkowicz.

★

How does a senior Fine Arts thesis project about the artist's experience of violation become a tool to damn her as, at best, a fame-seeker and, at worst, a liar?

★

This is one of the pernicious effects of patriarchal culture: we are taught to mistrust the testimony of those who have endured rape. We are taught not to trust the women. We are taught immediately to doubt the instant that an accused man says, *but I am a feminist*, or simply that the accuser is lying.[25] More specifically, what the media representation of Emma Sulkowicz exemplifies is one of the most insidious effects of patriarchy: rape culture.

★

Enter the feminist killjoy.

---

25. Nungesser made this claim in a statement to *New York Times* columnist Ariel Kaminer. See <http://www.nytimes.com/2014/12/22/nyregion/accusers-and-the-accused-crossing-paths-at-columbia.html?>.

Killing the joys of patriarchal culture means asking whose impunity is guaranteed. And then it means responding clearly: the impunity of those who enact violences, small and large, that are fostered and fetishized by patriarchal culture. And it is hard work. Look again at Emma Sulkowicz—a young woman, an artist, a fourth-year university student, a person who has endured rape, an activist, a public intellectual. First, she and her work make the rounds on social and mainstream media to relatively positive reception. Then, after her accused rapist states that he is a feminist, she is cast as a liar and attention-seeker.

What Emma Sulkowicz's experience and her project *Carry That Weight* remind us is that we do not know how to talk about rape culture in a productive, generative, and healing manner. Instead, because the work of restorative justice is hard, because unlearning patriarchal culture is hard, we tend to fall into cycles of blaming and shaming again and again and again. This return to damaging gender-based scripts is devastating for women, devastating for men, and devastating for any chance at an equitable future.

*

El Jones, a spoken word artist, writer, activist, teacher, and former Poet Laureate of Halifax, Nova Scotia, where I live (and, full disclosure, my friend), recently wrote about how we *can't* talk about rape and rape culture. She was writing specifically about the ways in which women's testimony has been used against them in the case against former Canadian Broadcasting Corporation (CBC) host Jian Ghomeshi, whom I'll speak more about soon. El observed how women tend to speak about rape and rape culture in online space. There, she notes, *women have forged online spaces to process sexual assault and trauma.*[26] Digital space is, as El notes, one place where one woman's statement of factual affect—*I couldn't look at him,* for example—is recognized and validated by other women rather than interrogated for objective and evidentiary support.

Because we believe white supremacist patriarchal language and expression is normal, right, and the only way of understanding meaning, we believe the way language is interpreted by the law must be correct. The fact that language use is cultural, gendered, and classed, means that meaning—and misunderstanding—is imposed on those who do not express themselves in the manner dictated by straight white European upper class men. When this meaning is imposed on others, it leads to reading guilt, or lack of remorse, or other projections on those who do not share this expression. Understanding that white male approved language is not THE language but also a cultural expression of one group—no better or more important than any other except by their ability to impose it on everyone else—is important also in seeking justice. Injustice is encoded not just in systems, but literally in how we talk about them, what words and whose words count, and who defines truth for other people.[27]

---

26. El Jones, Facebook Status Update, March 1, 2016.

27. Ibid.

Look at the way that El Jones identifies how one mode of communication gets taken up as the *de facto* proper mode and how this delegitimizes other ways of knowing. Validation of your own feelings and experiences. Imagine. What a thing!

★

Actually, we don't have to imagine it, we can look for specific examples.

For instance, in the fall of 2014, Antonia Zerbisias and Sue Montgomery created the hashtag #BeenRapedNeverReported for social media circulation. The hashtag idea came about after news broke of the much-beloved CBC radio host Jian Ghomeshi's alleged sexual assaults of several women. Instead of focusing on the accusations, critics asked why women hadn't reported the assaults earlier.

Are you fucking kidding me? I mean, that would have been my gut response. It *was* my gut response. But Zerbisias and Montgomery had a more level-headed way to call attention to that degrading and patronizing question. They started tweeting in support of women who have been raped and had never reported their assault.

On October 31, 2014, Sue Montgomery (@MontgomerySue) tweeted: *He was a senior flight attendant. I was a sum-*

mer flight student. Learned later there had been many victims. #BeenRapedNeverReported

And

He was my grandfather. I was 3-9 yo. Cops wanted to know why I waited so long to report it. #BeenRapedNeverReported

And on October 30, 2014, Antonia Zerbisias (@AntoniaZ) tweeted: *#ibelievelucy #ibelievewomen And yes, I've been raped (more than once) and never reported it. #BeenRapedNeverReported*

And

It was 1969 when, if you found you were the only girl in the rec room and no parents were home, it was your fault. #BeenRapedNeverReported

Mainstream culture—that is to say white patriarchal culture—purports to talk about rape and rape culture in objective terms. But really, these terms are not objective. As El Jones points out, the so-called "objective" language of mainstream culture does not make room for emotion, affect, relational thinking, or colloquialism. Instead, it demands that the speaker use neutrality (as though there were such a thing), objectivity (as though objectivity were a fact, not an ambition), and logic (despite there being a plurality of logics that coexist alongside patriarchal logic).

We are taught to dismiss or be wary of any language that can be read as feminized or, for that matter, racialized. So maybe we have, through Jones's thinking, come to a reason for why digital space has become an incredible site of solidarity for women, people of colour, queer, and trans people to talk. Digital space is a habitually colloquial space. Testimonial space. A space quite literally engineered for excess, for connectivity, for intersectionality and linked thinking.

And perhaps the conversational, emotional language that circulates so fluidly in digital space also demonstrates Audra Williams's claim. Perhaps that conversational, emotional, complex discourse of the text message or the tweet conveys the spiderweb-intricacy of trying to work out your experience of violence, while simultaneously trying to keep control of your own narrative.

> *lol yusss*
>
> *Also I feel like we need to have some real time where we can talk about life and thingz because we still haven't really had a paul-emma chill sesh since summmmmerrrr*

Freeze. Appease. Mend. Tend. Befriend.

*

Women are more likely to trivialize their experiences. Women are more likely to use backchannels (emailing, using social media, talking, writing shitlists)[28] to alert one another to potentially harmful situations or to circulate stories of inequity.

★

Recognizing, addressing, and changing long-standing systemic issues takes time, and in a hyper-mediated world, slow thinking is not something that is particularly valued. It is, however, something that is necessary. I'm interested in first opening a discussion about how to sustain slow, deliberate, and public thinking about issues of misogyny, rape culture, and asymmetrical power relations in the face of the rapid-fire pace of social media.

How are we working to sustain slow thinking about these pressing issues in a public way? "Public" here is key, I think. Publicness is not a fail-safe—often for women it is the opposite—but it does keep attention on a topic maybe, just maybe, long enough to shake the systemic conditions that sustain inequity.

★

Is it any wonder that the hashtag #BeenRapedNeverReported went viral?

---

28. See, for example, Antonia Zerbisias (who co-founded #BeenRapedNeverReported) on the rise of the shitlist as a feminist warning system. "Feminism's Fourth Wave is the Shitlist," *Now [Toronto]* 16 Sept 2015 <https://nowtoronto.com/news/feminisms-fourth-wave-is-the-shitlist/>.

*

Actually, the real question I have is this: Why are we not *all* listening to, learning from, and, most importantly, supporting Lucy DeCoutere in her activist endurance?[29]

*

How am I going to teach him not to rape?

How am I going to teach her about rape without teaching her to be afraid all the time?

My friend H. and I are sitting on the floor, legs wide, feet nearly touching, in the doorway between her living room and dining room. We're sitting on a series of interlocking, brightly coloured foam tiles. Between us, E. and E. are picking things up and putting them down. These are our babies, a boy and a girl. My girl is a month older than H.'s boy. They are fascinating, these little creatures. One picks up a block and waves it seriously in the air. The other looks up, smiles a gummy smile, and goes back to concentrating on hitting a spatula against a small drum. They are eight and nine months' old.

---

29. Lucy DeCoutere is a captain in the Royal Canadian Air Force. She is also an actor who is perhaps best known for her work in Trailer Park Boys. In October 2014, she and seven other women spoke publicly about being sexually assaulted by then-CBC host Jian Ghomeshi. DeCoutere was the first of the women to allow for her name to be revealed to the public, and the only witness in the trial to allow her name to be public. She is a goddamn hero.

H. and I have been getting to know one another in this doorway over the past several months. We've both spent a great deal of our lives thus far writing and reading. This feels new, this constant movement and noise and distraction. New, good, amazing, hard, maddening, and paradoxical. As our infants squeak, squawk, yowl, coo, and spit up, we talk. It's a new kind of talk, one that we're both getting used to as we also become familiar and then comfortable with one another. Conversation is fragmented, urgent, constantly interspersed with shifts in attention from each other to these two creatures ooching about between us. The first time we met like this, I left exhausted and thrilled, with the sense that I had quite possibly talked too much too fast. I couldn't wait to go back the next week. As we sit on the floor between the dining room and the living room, we watch the babies grow less wobbly, week by week. We try to keep them from bumping into the hard edges of the doorway.

*

How am I going to teach him not to rape?
How am I going to teach her about rape without teaching her to be afraid all the time?

*

I don't know. I don't know. That's what we've come up with so far, H. and I. That we don't have the language yet to say quite what we mean, much less to talk to our kids about it when the time comes. And the time will come, fast.

I wonder if they taught boys in Grade Nine sex ed not to rape. H. asked this, rhetorically, as the babies both reached for a rainbow tangle of large, wooden blocks. *I mean, I remember two-thirds of Sex Ed. being about how not to get raped.*

Not me, I replied. *In my high school in rural North Carolina, we were taught abstinence was the only way to keep from getting pregnant. Forget getting raped, too much heavy petting and you were up the spout, reputation ruined forever. If you were a girl, I mean.* If you were a girl.

We laugh ruefully about this, H. and I, but we keep coming back to the questions that don't feel quite right in the phrasing, yet are deeply urgent in our concern and intent. We want to do well for these creatures. We want to prepare them without hardening them. We haven't said this to each other, but I think we want to give them what we didn't have ourselves. We want, I think, to be hopeful that things will change, and to be part of that changing.

*

I once saw a mural by contemporary Australian artist Brad Buckley. The piece is from Buckley's larger *Slaughterhouse Project*, which curator Brett Levine describes as a suite of works *which calls into question the roles and responsibilities of cultures to consider and address diverse concerns.*[30] The piece

30. Brett Levine, 'Princes Kept the View' catalogue essay for *The Slaughterhouse Project: The Light on the Hill*, Visual Arts Gallery, University of Alabama at Birmingham, USA (2002) in Brad Buckley, John Conomos, Australian Centre for Photography, 2013, 51–59.

was formed of the word "HOPE" hovering in bright red letters over a group of human silhouettes. Never mind, for the moment, that Levine is talking about contemporary art and I am talking about rape culture; in both cases, hope gets harnessed in service of *something*. Abstract, that word *something*, isn't it?

Doing something, in Ahmed's estimation, is as an impossible demand, one that is often framed as a question (*what can I do?*). Impossible, but imperative. We need to ask impossible questions, she claims, because impossible questions are future-oriented ones. *The future is both a question mark and a mark of questioning*, writes Ahmed. *The question of the future is an affective one; it is a question of hope for what we might yet be, as well as fear for what we could become.*[31] Indeed, writing this is an attempt *to do something*.

But what can we do? What can I do?

I'm not unfamiliar with a kind of optimistic hope being harnessed as a politically and personally affective tool. Like the slogan "Change," "Hope" has been imbued with relentlessly positive, outward-reaching characteristics, what Ernst Bloch describes as a broadening out of the self.[32] As I turned to Buckley's large-scale mural, these senses of hope turned with me.

---

31. Sara Ahmed, *The Cultural Politics of Emotion* (New York: Routledge, 2004) 183–84.

32. Ernst Bloch, *The Principle of Hope* (Vol. 1), trans. Neville Plaice, Stephen Plaice, and Paul Knight (Oxford: Blackwell, 1986) 3.

But guess what? Buckley's mural has a subtitle. *HOPE*, it reads, *is still a four-letter word.*

Anna Potamianou posits that hope can work as a kind of roadblock, something that would get in the way of doing something.[33]

*

Is what H. and I are reaching for actually hope?

*

I suspect where we find ourselves stuck, is, in fact, not hope in the traditional sense, but a new iteration of the affect gone wild: again Lauren Berlant's *cruel optimism.* Cruel optimism is a relational situation that exists when *something you desire is actually an obstacle to your flourishing.*[34] That thing you want might not be cruel in and of itself, but it becomes so when *the object that draws your attachment actively impedes the aim that brought you to it initially.* For Berlant, optimism does not always feel *good*, but it is an attachment with an affective structure. Whether it manifests in anxiety, stress, or hope, an optimistic attachment requires you to return again and again to the scene of the fantasy of what you desire with

33. Anna Potamianou, *Hope: A Shield in the Economy of Borderline States.* Trans. Philip Slotkin (London: Routledge, 1997) 79.

34. Berlant 4.

the belief that somehow, this time, it will be different and things will be better.

The optimism is cruel, Berlant explains, when the object that lights you with the sense of hopeful possibility forecloses the very possibility that you will take the actions necessary to make attaining that desired thing a real possibility.

In this case, the thing we want—some different, rape-free future—is impeded by our hoping. Hear me out: Hope, here, is another subset of patriarchal culture. Like the making strange of rape, hope isn't an action; it's an impediment to action.

Here's what I mean:

What if H. and I asked the questions differently? What if, instead of *How am I going to teach him not to rape; how am I going to teach her about rape without teaching her to be afraid all the time,* we put the questions this way:

How am I going to make sure that he isn't taught to rape? How am I going to make sure that she isn't taught to be afraid at a cellular level?

The difference between these questions and the original ones is that they presume a different future is actually possible. Both my friend and I were assuming the inevitabilities of rape culture in our infants' lives. And that's understandable. We've learned those narratives and inevitabilities ourselves. They've become our frames of reference. That's the joy that needs killing: the sense of inevitability, that sense that rape—doing it or having it done to you—is somehow an inevitable, ever-present reality. Shifting our questions shifts our action, energies, and affects from within (I hope, I hope, I worry, I fret) to *with each other*. We move from the internalization of rape and rape culture as inevitable towards dialogue with others that positions rape, rape culture, gendered violence, and the associated traumas, big and small, as sites of struggle.

*

I believe that rape, trauma, and gendered violence are sites of struggle.... talking is the only way to move forward. And I believe that this talking brings us more than just the strength to "go on"; I believe that it will bring change. Not quickly. Not without discomfort. But it will.

.... I talk about the labor of talking about rape, and one of the points I make is how important it is to break the silence around rape, because the silence (born of guilt, trauma, and shame) gives the rapes and the rapists more power. In that way, I believe that talking about gendered violence is an inherently political act.[35]

*

Talking. Telling stories. Trying to put it into words. That's

---

35. Troyan, "The Body Always Remembers."

what I'm after. Trying to find the right words to say these things so that they are heard by people who don't already know, all day, every day, that we live in a rape culture and that it affects us all, differently. Trying to find the words to name things that my body knows, that my friends' bodies know, but which we've never been able to say without being questioned, or shamed, or made to feel defensive. Trying to say these things so clearly as to be irrefutable. Trying to say them so that there is no room for argument and only room for action.

*

It's hard, this trying. Even drawing on the fierce archive of writing, theory, and testimony is hard. I feel these stories on my skin and in my body. I feel my own traumas, small and less small, surfacing as exhaustion, as short-temperedness fired out at my partner when, after hours at the computer, I still haven't gotten it right. I feel it in my bones and in the throbbing that begins over my left eyebrow, where a large crease bears witness to the face I make when I'm trying to be calm and clear. When I fear my emotions might somehow dilute my clarity.

*

Amy Berkowitz has written about the difficulty of putting experiences of gender-based trauma into words. It's not only the significant challenge of returning to the somatic site of trauma that is difficult.[36] Berkowitz describes her own book, *Tender Points*, as one that plays around with masculine drag. She tells Cassandra Troyan, *early on I vow to write the book in "male" speech that will be taken seriously (declarative sentences, authoritative tone, lists, medical jargon), and this turns out to be a lie.*[37] Berkowitz's book, which is a lyric essay about her life lived with chronic pain and trauma borne of rape and rape culture, employs what she calls *écriture feminine en homme*. I love this phrase. *Écriture feminine*—writing in the feminine— is a term that was coined to describe the joyous, non-linear theory being written by French feminists such as Hélène Cixous, Luce Irigaray, and Julia Kristeva in the 1970s–80s. They were working to wrench theoretical writing from the austerity of academic language that was (is) associated with logic, whiteness, and masculinity. *Here I am in my body, writing*, they seem to say through the very syntax of their sentences and the structures of their unfurling thoughts. Their writing harnessed what Freud called hysteric symptoms—non-linearity, emotion, affect—in service of writing from a deliberately and self-consciously gendered position.

The atemporality, the "hysterical" and affective language, the non-linearity, the personal: all of these structural tactics become weapons of the feminist killjoy.

If, as my editor and friend J. says so astutely, *rape culture doesn't have a linear history* in either social memory or in

---

36. Understatement-of-the-year candidate, that sentence there.

37. Ibid.

our own biographies, then rape culture is atemporal and it requires atemporal, non-linear methods of putting words one after another to tell it and to tell it again. So if you find yourself automatically rejecting this, rejecting me as your interlocutor, take a moment to reflect on where the root of your rejection stems. From me? Or from the enormity of the joys that need killing?

*

As I write this, it has been more than a year and a hand-ful of days since the CBC fired Jian Ghomeshi. Do you remember how the news broke? I do. I remember seeing it on Twitter first and thinking *how strange*. And then, later that evening, I recall sitting on the couch with my partner. We were both looking at Facebook—oh, modern life—and came across Ghomeshi's long, bizarre, self-defensive post. Remember, that's the post in which he claimed that the CBC had fired him for his non-normative sexual preferences. I recall thinking at the time that there had to be more to the story. Further, I remember thinking here was someone who knew how gender plays a powerful role in public opinion. A well-known man confessing and apologizing for his less-than-vanilla proclivities, but asking for the public to respect his privacy? Wow, I thought. Very savvy.

And then the real story broke. "More to the story" turned out to be many, many women. Women who had experi-enced varying degrees of assault and harassment in professional, private, and semi-private settings. Women who did not feel safe coming forward and women who did not feel safe, but felt responsible for coming forward anyway.

I remember listening to Lucy DeCoutere being interviewed about her decision to talk publicly about her experience with Ghomeshi. I remember what she said—that she felt she could come forward, and so she did in hopes that it would make other women feel strong—but I mostly remember her voice. Confident. Assured. Strong in her own truth. And controlled. Oh, her voice was so controlled. And I remember thinking, *wow, this woman*. This woman and her bravery. She has brought her experience into the light of the public—not a warm light, that—for the good of other people. *How generous*, I thought. *Thank you*, I thought.

And then, of course, there was more. More women, yes, and more public backlash. The women who didn't come forward were asked why. They weren't even recipients of the question, not usually. Rather, there was a general distrust of anonymity and silence. Why wouldn't you come forward and seek justice, the whole country—never mind the comments' sections—seemed to ask, while simultaneously failing to make a connection with the myriad risks of doing so in public.

The conversations about Ghomeshi's years of violence were triggering. Talking and hearing about it non-stop was exhausting. And yet, it felt as though it was time for something to change. Would these conversations lead to a public recognition and outcry for an inquiry into the missing and murdered indigenous women and girls in Canada? Would it lead to cities and provinces changing their tack? Would universities and colleges start to take the persistence of rape culture on campuses seriously? Would public opinion shift to trusting women when they say they've been abused, assaulted, raped?

Something else did start to happen. Women reached out to one another. Again, I saw this happen first on social media. In my city, a group formed on the Internet to talk about how we were dealing with this hyper public, inescapable, necessary-yet-gutting conversation about rape culture. Then the #BeenRapedNeverReported hashtag went viral. Women all over the Internet were claiming their experiences of violence and teaching the general public not only *why* a huge percentage of sexualized violence goes unreported; they were also teaching us what that feels like. They were teaching us how violence that is both individualized and systematic—it happened to me, it happened within patriarchal culture, within racist culture, and so forth—gets metabolized or internalized. They were teaching us, these women. We were teaching each other.

*

This Changed Me. That was the title of an article published by *Chatelaine* one year after Ghomeshi was fired and news of his abuses broke.[38] In the article Sarah Boesveld notes,

The events of that day hit like a brick to a window—a "where were you when" moment for a great many Canadians. Regardless of how Ghomeshi's trial plays out in 2016, we're still feeling this scandal's repercussions a year later. It led to thousands of conversations about sexual violence, workplace harassment and abuses of power. For those at the core of it—the survivors who came forward, the CBC employees who lost their jobs and Ghomeshi's family—the fallout is ongoing and severe. But even for many further afield—crisis workers and policymakers, journalists and former colleagues—the scandal has had a powerful, lasting effect.

The article interviews seven women about the lasting effect of this public discussion of rape culture. They are all worth reading carefully. I'm struck, especially, by Piya Chattopadhyay's recollection of hosting *Q* the day the news broke, of how she is willing to admit how emotional she was. But I want to draw your attention to the last interview, which is with Sally Armstrong. *Immediately after the column, I had a phone call from a very well-known Canadian man with lots of connections. He said, "Pick a Saturday—any Saturday that doesn't have a Santa Claus Parade on it and I'll organize a march of the men." I said "I hope you do. I'd be willing to help." But I never heard from him again. It didn't surprise me because it takes a lot of effort to alter the status quo. The Jian Ghomeshi thing was an incident—that goes on in most offices across Canada today.*

38. Sarah Boesveld, "This Changed Me. The Lasting Impact of the Ghomeshi Scandal," *Chatelaine* 26 Oct 2015 <http://www.chatelaine.com/living/project97-living/the-lasting-impact-of-the-jian-ghomeshi-scandal/>.

And who's going to do something about it? And I don't believe a single incident has stopped because of the Jian Ghomeshi story.

Armstrong articulates what worries me so deeply about how we remember—as communities, as people. And as much as I am loath to admit it, I think, on a large scale, Armstrong is right.

But I don't want to end there, because on a smaller scale—and by small, I mean geographically smaller scale—things have happened. The public discussions of rape culture and misogyny did change me. It reminded me that I'm not just a teacher; I am, more specifically, a feminist teacher. I am not just a person at the front of a classroom, I am a gendered body at the front of the room. I have to negotiate power dynamics every day, of course, but this? This incident renewed my resolve to talk about rape culture, gendered and racial inequity, and the function of power dynamics in my classrooms: even when it makes me uncomfortable; even when it might mean that my student evaluations are chock full of comments that "she's too feminist"; even when it's risky.[39] It is my privilege and it is my responsibility to teach and write with a feminist lens. And so I do. I am. I'm trying.

---

39. And it *is* risky. One example from the time the *Chatelaine* article came out was, of course, the open threats of violence made to all feminists (especially feminist professors) on the University of Toronto campus. See Lily Cho's "Vulnerabilities" (<http://www.hookandeye.ca/2015/09/vulnerabilities. html>) for a good introduction to the context and the affect associated with this example.

*

And you know what? Something else happened, too. About two weeks after my baby was born, I went to a brunch held by the founder of that online feminist discussion group. The group, which was full of women in Halifax who care about feminism and each other, had spent a year navigating the emotional rapids that came about after the news of Ghomeshi's actions. It was a group of women who took the time to build a network of verbal support for one another in a space—the Internet—that feels so ephemeral, so risky. And while I was jittery about meeting them in person, and shy and awkward and full of all the weird hormones that come with giving birth, I went. And as I walked up the stairs to meet a group of women with whom I'd really only talked online, with my very wee girl in my arms, someone said, *Oh! A baby! Pass me that baby and get that woman a cup of coffee!*

And so, as I passed my daughter into this familiar stranger's arms, I whispered in my daughter's ear, *this is Lucy.*

Chapter 2:
Notes on Friendships

When I think of my childhood, I think of myself as solitary. No siblings (fine by me), no huge extended family. When I think of my childhood, I think of my parents, grandparents, and Great Aunt Bess. I don't think of childhood friends; I think of books I read in the car, in the living room, in small nooks and crannies of the house that I tried to make as magical as the garret room conjured by the imaginations of the small Victorian girls I was reading about.

*

My mother has recently remarked that I was an irrepressibly social baby. This surprises me, but she was there and taking more stock than I was, so I trust her.

*

Still, when I think of early friendships, I think not of people but of books. Books were my friends, and more often than not, the characters in the books were my imaginary friends, who stepped out of the pages and walked with me to school or sat in bed with me, talking when I was meant to be asleep. What I mean is, reading was my friend. And also I mean that I learned about friendship—patience, slowness, listening, care—from reading, and from reading about friendships between other people.

*

If writing and reading can be modelled on friendship, what sorts of friendships emerge between female writers and readers? And between what Maggie Nelson refers to as *the many-gendered mothers of my heart*?

*

When I think of my childhood friendships, I think of Jane and Maya and Sara and Tess, who lived in the pages of the books that I was always allowed to select from our large, inherited collection. I gravitated, first, towards books like *The Secret Garden* and *A Little Princess*. Books that I now can't help but read through the lens of class, race, and colonial violence. At the time, though, I admired the ingenuity of the girls who were the protagonists. I admired their pluck. I aspired to be plucky and resilient myself.

I imagined surviving in garrets and saving the day with my wit and hard work.

I learned how conversation could be a weapon of attack or defence (thanks, Jane Austen); how being seen by the world as an unconventional beauty ("ugliness," "plainness," me-ness) made subversive room for learning (thanks, Charlotte Brontë); how class-restricted movement could make you your own worst enemy (merci, Flaubert/Madame Bovary); how writing is a tool of memory and resistance (thank you for teaching me and keeping me company with your words, Anne Frank, Maya Angelou); and how wildness can be a kind of refusal (thank you, Emily Brontë).

I didn't just read the classics, though. Not by a long shot. Equally, I think, too, of Claudia and Stacey and Mary Anne and Kristy and Dawn. You know them, right? The main characters from Ann M. Martin's formative *The Babysitter's Club*. I was allowed to read these books grudgingly. Grudg-ingly, because I am a fast reader and these books were an investment. And me? I'd devour them in one sitting and come up for air desperate for more stories of girls from different backgrounds being friends and starting a business together. It was wildly beyond my everyday life, and I loved every second of it. Claudia, who was an artist (an artist!) and had style beyond measure and a magical grandmother named Mimi. Stacey, who was from New York City(!) and whose parents were divorced (like those of my friends in Ottawa; *unlike* my new friends' parents in North Carolina). Mary Anne, who was being raised by her father. Kristy, who was adjusting to a newly blended family. Dawn, who was a hippie from California. I haven't gone back and read these books since I was a child—I'm afraid they wouldn't hold up—but at the time I learned from them about style, business ethics, responsibility, personality management, and friendship.

Reading has been my most constant friend. And looking back now, I see that I *did* read books with predominantly female protagonists.

Many of these girls and women were lonely, though. What's that about? And why, despite my voracious and vociferous and rangy reading habits, did I rarely happen across narratives of strong female friendship? These questions frame the way I want to think through how we encounter and experience narratives of friendship between women outside the pages of books.

*

(I realize I'm doing this thinking, with you, in the pages a book.)

*

I hate most of the words used to describe friendship among women.

What is it about female friendship that inspires such insipid descriptors? I struggle to find a collective noun that fits my friends without itching in its not-quite-right fit. *My girls* (too infantilizing). *My crew* (I don't row, so…). *My gal pals* (sounds like a condition). *My tribe* (too new age–appropriative). *My bitches* (just no).

I quite like *my brilliant friends*, but then I'm still riffing on a book rather than drawing from common usage...[1]

Really, though, what is the right way to say *C.*, whom I call when I'm sad or happy, with whom I dance wildly in the kitchen to '90s riot grrrl compilations, who takes care of my baby so my partner and I can work? What is the right way to say *M.* and *A.*, without whom I would never be brave enough to write? How do I say *H.* and convey what her fierce and hilarious give-no-fucks text messages mean, especially on wobbly-in-my-soul days? How can I tell you what it means to get emails from *S.*, who writes of waves and mermaids and how to breath poetry underwater? How do I say *H. M.* and make you understand what it means when we text each other about writing deadlines and being working moms and feminists? What about *L.* who is a lifeline of support across mountain ranges and time zones all the way from the other salty coast. I could go on. I've been looking for the language to describe friendship among women to myself, but I haven't found it yet.

Why is that?

What do we resist when we resist finding or forging this lan-

---

[1]. *My Brilliant Friend* is the English translation of Elena Ferrante's novel *L'Amica Genial*.

guage? What do we lose when we don't have the language to name the communities of care that hold our heads above water and bring us back to ourselves?

Maybe this language—like new friendships—is yet to come. Like the way Jacques Derrida describes unconditional hospitality as the future to come—*l'avenir*—an impossibility that, nonetheless, must be sought, anticipated, and wished for. It's not as though friendship between women doesn't exist. Of course it does, in multiple forms.

And yet. And yet this is a collection of essays that documents different moments when the feminist killjoy pokes and prods at problematic narratives. And this feminist killjoy thinks there's room for thinking carefully about how friendship among women gets talked about. There's room for improvement.

That's my argument.

And: there are some good reasons for thinking about how female friendships get represented in mainstream culture. Maybe telling the story of my revelation—that friendship among women is crucial to surviving in patriarchal culture—will help me find that language. Maybe.

⋆

It all feels so tentative, talking about friendship among women. That's what I found myself thinking while on a flight recently. It feels tentative, partial, provisional. And it feels necessary.

Part of the necessity comes from the need to think through the negative ways in which friendships between women have been cast. In *Bad Feminist*, Roxanne Gay encourages her readers to let go of the idea that female friendships have to be rife with toxicity and competition, and I agree. I do. But that narrative of toxic female friendships is *popular*. I mean, Lena Dunham and the other writers of *Girls* have made an empire out of representing tropes of women's negativity and ambivalence towards other women. Sure, there are some beautiful moments, but mostly the female friendships in *Girls* rely heavily on women being unkind to other women. Who is served by the narrative of the mean girls? Not the women. Yet when I think through the relationships I've had with women throughout my life, I can see why there is a common, negative idea to jettison. The dense atmospheric pressure surrounding discourses of female friendship indicates an absence of nuanced language. I don't mean to suggest that there is no nuance in female friendship—at times I feel those friendships are all in the nuances—but that there is a lack of nuanced narratives about friendship among women. Recently, a yoga teacher of mine wrote that for a long time she felt less-than when she was with other women whom she admired. More stunningly still, she wrote of how, when she witnessed the accomplishments of other women, she felt jealousy or self-pity rather than joy for them. Thank you, *N.*, for writing those words in a public place, because when I read them

I felt a pang of recognition. I am not proud or pleased to announce here in type to you that I have felt (feel) these things, but I have. I do. So when I say, there is a dense atmospheric pressure around discourses of female friendship, what I mean is this: in a very large way, women's relationships with other women are complicated by patriarchal culture. Patriarchal culture depicts women as conniving, as mean-spirited, as frivolous. Female friendships are almost always presented as built on cattiness and competition with other women. In patriarchal culture, women go behind each other's backs in order to get men's attention. These are just some of the ways in which women's relationships with other women are complicated by patriarchal culture. The problem with narratives of friendships between women is that they are inherited. They get passed down and received as a matter of course: *This is how it goes between women.* That reception—indeed, the transmission of these narratives—is a mode of destruction and of patriarchal policing.

How women relate to themselves, much less other women, is a dense and often stifling process of feeling in the dark. Of feeling different kinds of darkness—some comforting, some dangerous. Some soft. Some prickling. And the ways in which the world talks about women—about friendships among women—complicates those unlit narratives further.

*

One of the things I feel most certain of these days is that the feminist killjoy can't go it alone. She needs friends. She needs a support network. She needs allies. She needs respite from the work of killing joy and making a world. This much I know to be true. And yet, in much the same way that I cringe when I think of past me, too smug and smart for feminism, I cringe when I tell you that it's taken me such a long time to wrap my head around why the feminist killjoy needs friendship with other women. We know that female friendship exists. We know that there are more iterations of it that would fit in any essay. Why, then, do we see, over and again, representations of female friendships that police those friendships into invisibility or strip them of their radical potential, until only a ghost of their reality is left hovering in the margins? What would female friendship as a way of life look like?

*

Let's think about some of the places where these blunted stories of women's friendship circulate. I don't want to be all "kids-these-days-with-their-Internet," especially because that stance suggests that adults aren't constantly plugged in, too (besides, screen-time *is* a feminist issue…).[2] Nor do I want to shake my finger at "mainstream media" or "pop culture," as though I'm some highbrow intellectual who claims never to have heard of Beyoncé and has no memory of the double-rainbow guy on YouTube. Rather,

---

2. Jessica Michaelson, "Screen-Time is a Feminist Issue," *DRJESSICAMI-CHAELSON* 18 Aug 2015 <http://www.drjessicamichaelson.com/blog/screen-time-feminist>.

what I mean is that there's something compelling about the multiple modes in which pop culture moves in our current moment. So let's start there.

*

When I think pop culture, the first things that come to mind are those television shows and movies from when I was younger. I don't think of Raymond Williams's insightful argument that culture is ordinary, nor do I immediately conjure up the Frankfurt School theorists. Rather, I think about *My So-Called Life*, *The Jerry Springer Show*, and *Nikita*. I think about Baz Luhrmann's *Romeo + Juliet*. Why the strange archive, you may ask? Why indeed? The answer is simple: These are the television shows (and one movie) that I watched in first-year university, huddled around my suite-mate's television with seven other women.

I went to a big state school in the southern United States. My suite-mates hailed from Alabama, other parts of North Carolina, Georgia, Massachusetts, and one came from North Carolina by way of the American School in London. We were white and we were black. We were all in our first year of university. Not many of us were friends outside the dorm; we broke off into our own groups as we started to find our way out of the rush of being university students. I lost track of all but one of my suite-mates by second year, though we would smile and chat if we ran into one another on campus.

But for that first year when we were in the suite together, we took care of one another, after a fashion.

We listened to issues with boys, classes, and families. We checked in on one another when we got sick, and get sick we did. I had a chronic condition that landed me in the hospital every few months, writhing in pain and hooked up to IVs. I distinctly remember being discharged the first time and not knowing how I would get back to the dorm. It was a twenty-minute walk, and I could hardly stand. Suddenly, in came A. and D. They had talked a Point-to-Point driver into coming to pick me up. They bundled me into the van, got me back to the dorm, and we sat down to watch television. Someone made me Cup-Noodles.

Actually, only some of us watched re-runs of *My So-Called Life* and *Nikita*, but for one semester we all seemed to gather together to watch *The Jerry Springer Show*. What I remember best about this was the deep pleasure we derived from watching garbage television mixed with a vague but unshakable sense that something was really wrong about the whole thing. I realize now that there were *a lot* of things wrong with *The Jerry Springer Show*—its facilitations of white paternalism, of classed and raced stereotypes, and of narrow and reductive narratives for women, to name but a few. But I particularly remember one afternoon when D. said to everyone and no one in particular, *I don't know why these women are hating on each other; that slack-ass man is the one who cheated on them both.*

And there it was.

Just like that, D. named the vague discomfiture that we were all feeling: Why did the women have to scream, fight, pull each other's hair, and smash furniture on the stage while the cheating-ass boyfriend sat back, arms crossed, smirking? Just what-the-actual-fuck was that all about? So that's what I think about when I think of pop culture: those ubiquitous sites of cultural reference that permeate our everyday lives whether we pay attention to them or not. Pop culture, I wager, is a fine place to keep us thinking about how narratives of women's friendship (not to mention hateship à la Jerry Springer) circulate.

Critics of pop culture point out that it would be a mistake to suggest that so-called lowbrow or middlebrow cultural production has no effect on how we think about how we move through the world. One such critic, Anita Sarkeesian, does an especially amazing job of pointing to the limited and flat-footed ways in which pop culture portrays women. Sarkeesian is the founder of *The Feminist Frequency*, which began as a series of YouTube videos in which she analyzed either the available narratives for women in video games or did quick, accessible Bechdel Tests on films.

[By the way, if you're not familiar with the Blechdel test it is both amazingly useful and, often, results in a sense of vertigo. Alison Bechdel popularized the test in her comic *Dykes to Watch Out For*. The test is straightforward. To pass, a movie needs to have:

1) At least two named women in it;
2) the named women characters need to talk to each other; and
3) the named women characters need to talk to each other about something other than a man.

Seems simple, right? Wrong. As Sarkeesian points out over and over again, even films that appear to boast strong female characters and feminist or pop-feminist storylines often fail the test. Oh, and here's a fun fact: Sarkeesian has received death threats, bomb threats, and has had to cancel public speaking events. Why, you ask? Because some people, gathered under the umbrella of hatred called #Gamergate, are so deeply threatened by her analysis of gendered narratives in pop culture, and especially video game culture, that threats of bodily violence are their version of so-called rational engagement with the thinking of another.

Lest we forget that being a feminist killjoy is also, often, risky. Lest we forget that the "joys" that need killing are the so-called joys of patriarchal culture. Lest we forget how much the world needs feminist killjoys.]

*

All right, let's think through pop culture representations of gendered relationships with an eye towards women's friendships. While I was on a plane—the same flight that had me thinking about female friendship in the first place—I decided to watch a movie. The movie I chose was *The Intern*

(2015), written and directed by Nancy Meyers. The premise of the film sounds promising, if a bit silly: Ben, a 70-year-old widower played by Robert De Niro, decides he's bored with retirement and becomes an intern to Jules, a young, wildly successful Internet business-owner played by Anne Hathaway. This is not the stuff of my cinematic dreams—for one thing, the entire film could be a contender for #OscarsSoWhite—but I was on a flight and wanted some background noise, most of the other choices were shoot-'em-up films, and this looked tolerable.[3] So I watched it.

The film surprised me. It had all the earmarks of a fluffy-blockbuster: precocious children; affluent characters bopping about in casually expensive outfits; (mostly) inoffensive age-based humour (Ben poses formally while the younger interns flash peace signs for Instagram, for example); and ruffled thirty-somethings trying to be adults. The central characters, Ben and Jules, are likeable. Ben, the "fairy god-father" of the film, is an insightful, non-threatening older white guy who manages to wow all the twenty- or thirty-somethings with his life experience.[4] Jules is brilliant, self-

3. The hashtag #OscarsSoWhite was created by April Reign in protest of the complete lack of racial diversity in the nominees. Reign has created a really super ten-point plan for change, beginning with the DuVernay test, which requires that two actors of colour have "fully realized lives," rather than "serving as scenery in white stories." See <https://www.theguardian.com/film/2016/feb/25/oscarssowhite-10-point-plan-hashtag-academy-awards-april-reign>.

4. Richard Brody calls Ben's character a "fairy godfather" in his review "'The Intern' is a Very Strange Workplace Fantasy," *The New Yorker* 25 Sept 2015 <http://www.newyorker.com/culture/richard-brody/the-intern-is-a-very-strange-workplace-fantasy>.

doubting, beautiful, and slightly frosty; all markers, I'd suggest, of what it takes to be seen as a successful woman in mainstream culture.

Anyway, the two become friends, and what surprised me the most was that the narrative resisted some of the plot points I was expecting. Ben and Jules don't have anything other than a friendship. Indeed, he's the one she confides in when, in the midst of her business taking off, her husband, who gave up his career to be a stay-at-home dad, has an affair. Many (if not all) of my expectations around pop culture representations of heteronormative relationships were happily unmet. So what's wrong with this film?

It finally hit me: Jules has *no female friends whatsoever*.

Instead, she's got a predictably toxic relationship with her mom, who is only ever a voice on a telephone telling Jules that she's at risk of getting wrinkled and fat if she keeps working too hard. And she has a slightly abusive relationship with Robin, her administrative assistant, who in turn feels underappreciated by Jules and winds up weeping in the arms of one of the male interns. Oh, and there are Jules's brutal interactions with the stay-at-home moms from her daughter's school. These women—drab beside Jules's high fashion and bright lipstick—are incisive in their judgment of her work and scathing in their criticism of her inability to find time to make—rather than buy—snacks for their children's birthday parties. At one point Jules sighs, *Seriously? It's 2015. Are we still judgmental about working mothers?*

(Aside: this statement of Jules's made me LOL on the plane—a cardinal sin, public laughing while alone. I laughed rather than have a small weep because our recently minted Canadian prime minister had just gone viral on the Internet for saying, simply, *because it is 2015*, in response to the question *why is gender parity important?*

Mic drop.

The Internet died of joy and amazement. And I did too, sure, because it *matters* to have someone in power—someone such as the Right Honourable Justin Trudeau, with his whiteness and his privilege and his power and his politics and his awareness of how media moves mountains—say this.

But when a woman laments gender inequity? Silence. Eye-rolling. Exhaustion.)

Back to Jules and her stay-at-home mean-girl foils.

This storyline of the perfect/drab/child-focused moms drops out of the film shortly after these women judge Jules and her store-bought guacamole. The viewer is left only with the trace of their dissatisfaction and their smugness. Also, these women don't even interact with each other. These moms are not allowed individuality or nuance. They are only ever on screen together, a dyad dressed in twin-sets, giving Jules dirty looks or trying to shame Ben, who is babysitting Jules's daughter. Vapours of that dense barometric pressure.

*

While Jules becomes flustered by these catty caricatures of women, Ben shrugs them off with ease. In addition to reifying the authority of a single, senior, white man, *The Intern* recapitulates the narrative of the isolated woman and toxic female relationships, and it once again casts a woman with drive and ambition as both shrew and fool. The take-away from this film is that Jules manages to keep her business because her mentor—the intern who arrives *after* her business is a success, I might add—is an older fellow with life experience. Further, from mainstream culture's perspective, you can either be a mean, overbearing, child-obsessed bitch/mother or you can be a successful, frosty, shrewish, self-doubting, overbearing bitch/mother. *Great.*

This film, which is clearly working to present a progressive narrative of women (albeit white, upper-middle-class women), relies on a revised boy + girl calculus. Sure, Ben and Jules have a beautiful intergenerational friendship, and that matters. But why create this friendship at the cost of any meaningful female interactions *whatsoever*? Do we really not have better stories to tell?

*

Do we have no language to tell the stories of women's communities, not to mention women's friendship? Of course we do. When I crowdsourced a list of famous female friendships, the submissions defied my sense that there's no archive of women's communities and friendships. The list, gathered on Twitter and Facebook, included Virginia Woolf and Katherine Mansfield, Gertrude Stein and Sylvia Beach, Ann Friedman and Aminatou Sow (of the podcast *Call Your Girlfriend*), Calamity Jane and Dora DuFran, Margaret Laurence and Adele Wiseman, Ray Strachey and Millicent Garrett Fawcett (cross-generational suffragism FTW), Phryne Fisher and Dot Williams (of the series *Miss Fisher's Murder Mysteries*), Nina Simone and Miriam Makeba, Maggie Smith and Judi Dench, Nicki Minaj and Rihanna, the women of Bikini Kill, and Dorothy, Rose, Blanche, and Sophia of *The Golden Girls*. The lists went on.

*

And yet, when I think of my own experiences of friendships with women, there are so many places where those toxic narratives that Roxanne Gay mentions have seeped in. Why?

*

One of my first really formative memories of friendship with women was actually friendship with girls. And it was bad. It was Margaret-Atwood-*Cat's-Eye* bad, with all of the vague vicissitudes of ambivalent interactions and malevolent inflections that reverberate through decades of one's life, despite the work you might do to exorcise those ghosts. In fact, it has all the markers of an after-school special on adolescence, bullying, and outsider status.

It went something like this:

When I was eleven, my parents and I moved from Ottawa to rural North Carolina. My father, who worked on Parliament Hill as a chief of staff, burned out (actually, my mother recently told me that he was one of the first-diagnosed cases of chronic fatigue syndrome in Ottawa, though I have no statistics or evidence to back that up). So, after spending the first decade of my life in an urban centre—which at that point meant I had just been allowed my own library card—we moved to the country.

And I mean *country*. Yes, there were no neighbours in sight. But forget neighbours; there wasn't even a neighbourhood in the way that I understood it: no sound of kids playing hockey in the street; no walking to my best friend M.'s house; no daily trip to the Sportsplex for synchronized swimming lessons. Suddenly, everything was far away. It was nearly five kilometres to the convenience store. I remember walking there for the first time with my mother, in the hundred-percent-humidity heat, marvelling at the kudzu vines in the ditch and rehearsing my argument to drink an entire American-sized pop (now to be called soda to fit in). And school was now a half-hour drive across back roads and the Interstate into the closest town.

I started my new school when I was entering the sixth grade.

Let's not mince words: sixth graders can be awful humans, most especially to one another. I was in school before the discourse and awareness around bullying emerged, but that's what we were—a bunch of bullies. I say "we" here not because I was popular or, particularly, a bully, but I would have been if it had afforded me a bit of relief from the loneliness and strangeness of being new and of being the new girl.

As I crossed the Mason-Dixon Line, I left behind a group of friends who were kids and fell in with a group of new class-mates who were practically teenagers; they were more sexu-alized and socially savvy than anyone I had ever encountered who was my age. Maybe that's the difference a summer makes when you're eleven going on twelve. I don't know. What I do know is that I landed smack dab in the middle of sixth-grade politics. My first year in North Carolina, I was the new girl and the Canadian (both fine), the pledge (think being hazed for a sorority you didn't know existed), the minion in a popular girl's gang, the object of ridicule (one day, immediately and utterly, with no explanation), and the nerd whom everyone ignored. I was called a bitch, a slut, and a kiss-up. I learned that all the boys thought I was a slut, and there were all kinds of whispered conversa-tions about how far I would go and with whom. Here's the thing about slut-shaming: it is damning. And when you're young, lonely, and lacking the language to talk about this thing with *anyone* (hence "shame"), it is personally toxic.

★

I was lucky, in a way. Rather than falling deeply into self-harm and its various forms, I retreated into a performative discourse of passing. What I mean is: I learned really, really quickly how to practice self-surveillance, how to assess another girl for her potential threat, and how to feel constantly less-than and precarious in my friendships.

★

The most blatant obstacle to female friendship is the prevailing patriarchal adage that "women are each other's worst enemies."[5] That's Janice Raymond from her 1983 book *A Passion for Friends: Toward a Philosophy of Female Affection*. She goes on to say that this adage has all sorts of iterations, many of which are variations on Jonathan Swift's claim that he *never knew a tolerable woman to be fond of her own sex.*

Um, piss off, Jonathan. What kinds of damage has this bleak refrain wrought?

Back to Raymond, who has rather a lot to say on this point. For her, the damages are palpable, systemic, and devastating: *By blaring the hetero-relational message that "women are each other's worst enemies," men have ensured that many women will be each others' worst enemies. The obstacles to female friendship get good press. The message functions as a constant noise pollution in women's lives and is heard in many different places. Constant*

5. Janice G. Raymond, *A Passion for Friends: Toward a Philosophy of Female Affection* (North Melbourne: Spinifex Press, 1983) 151.

noise about women not loving women is supplemented by the historical silence about women always loving women.[6]

Raymond models a feminist killjoy critique here. By naming the systems—these "hetero-relational messages"—she's able to give her readers firm ground to stand on. Hetero-relational messaging tells women that they shouldn't like other women. It tells women that they aren't smart if they like other women. It tells women they should be spending their time pleasing and entertaining and seeking the company of men. Anything else is folly, it would seem. Think Betty and Veronica of the Archie Comics. One blond and girl-next-door, the other brunette and bitchy and fancy. They are cast as best friends, but really they're rivals for Archie's affections. This is hetero-relational messaging. This "constant noise pollution" becomes the backdrop against which women move through the world. And we know how pollution works: it seeps into everything it touches, permeating us with its toxins.

*

But then I read Raymond's earlier book, *The Transsexual Empire: The Making of the She-Male* (1979) and recoil. Her reprehensible transphobia hit me like a punch in the stomach and made me rethink everything I thought I'd learned from her book on friendship. In *The Transsexual Empire*, Raymond's thesis is this: transsexualism recapitulates gender

6. Ibid. 152.

and sexuality norms. For Raymond, not only does transitioning from the body you're born with into the body you know is yours constitute an affront on feminist gains, but it also reinforces gender stereotypes.

(Think, for example, of Kit, in the friend-filled series *L Word*, saying to Max just before his top surgery that he was mutilating his body and that butch identity should be enough, or of Alice refusing to include Max on her website because she didn't want to get flack from her lesbian viewers for having a trans man on the site.)[7]

And then, after basically writing the book on trans-exclusionary radical feminists, Raymond writes a book on friendship among women.

*

Raymond doubled back, and I'm disappointed and left wondering: Do I reject everything about what she says above that I found so useful?

Her polemic against trans-people undoes, for me, much of what I respect about her ability to name systemic violence.

*

---

7. Much has been written about the mishandling of trans-identity by the writers of the series. See, for example, <http://www.gender-focus.com/2012/04/27/neither-fish-nor-fowl-the-l-word-and-the-t-word/>.

How quickly we are recapitulated into the same systems that we try to dismantle.

I am disappointed by the friend I thought I found in her writing. Not all friendships are meant to last, I suppose. Not even with books.

*

My wariness around other women—my wariness around myself—lasted longer than I would like to admit. I felt that there were competing narratives of what female friendships are, and I didn't yet have the intellectual and emotional tools to manage them. What I had were too many experiences of ferociously close friendships with women that, for one reason or another, fell apart. It was as though we would get too close, too dependent on one another, and one day, suddenly, the barometric pressure of the relationship would shift, and just like that, drift would happen.

The drift is, I think, a facet of that hetero-relational messaging Raymond names (and, possibly, gets caught up in herself). I want close friendships with women. I'm drawn to them, and drawn into them. Most women I know want friendships with other women, too. Yet so often I've heard women say (and have said myself?) that it's easier to be friends with men. Great! I have wonderful friends who happen to be men, too. But in those anecdotal asides, I hear ambivalent hetero-relational messaging. It goes something like this: *Women make bad friends because they are jealous, vain, and insipid beings. Stupid, too. Women are stupid, and who wants a stupid friend?*

The effect of hetero-relational messaging—the micro- and macro-aggressions that seep in—is this: women are alienated from their own experiences of the world. They're told time and again that they don't matter, are less relevant, should take up less space, should be less hysterical, more thin less fat, etc., etc., etc. As women, we have to fight to reach a place of acceptance of our own being in the world.

Is it too hard to write your own narrative and witness another's, simultaneously? Is there a mirror stage here? When you're fighting to disregard all that hetero-relational messaging, is it occasionally too hard to witness a friend doing the same thing? Is that why some friendships between women crash into each other, noses pressed against glass, waving with wild recognition at the person on the other side, and then recede with the same force? Too much, too close, too similar, too uncanny?

*

In the old psychoanalytic telling, the mirror stage is a crucial moment in childhood development. The infant, who heretofore has experienced the world as this really awesome series of connected edges, voices, bodies, and comforts, suddenly has that sense of connectedness put into focus. One day, upon looking in the mirror and seeing another baby, then realizing that baby is *herself*, the infant's sense of connection and trust shifts ever so slightly, ever so profoundly: *Ah! That reflection in the mirror is and is not me! I experience the world from my own place in it, but there's an outer version of me that others read, and perhaps misread. How strange. How lonely.* From that point on, the infant knows both that she is separate from all other beings in the world (nascent loneliness) and that she is seen differently from how she sees herself (more nascent loneliness). This knowledge becomes either a burden or something else entirely.

Is seeing another woman living in patriarchy an experience of the mirror stage again? Does this reimagining of a second mirror state help to explain the toxicity that plays out in narratives of female friendship?

*

There are points in female friendship *where the intimacy and witnessing become too much both for the world in which it exists and for the language of the world as it is.* Sometimes witnessing someone else navigating the barrage of damage that patriarchal culture heaps on her while trying to navigate your own way is so very hard. It's hard to name all the ways in which you're oppressed by a system when it's the system you've been born into. And it's hard to watch someone else go through such similar oppressions. How does one imagine an outside to the culture we live in? How does one keep from getting too tired? How do we help and bear witness for another person when we have no idea how to do that work?

*

Perhaps drift happens when one friend in the equation has broken free from some binding narrative of patriarchal normativity, and that freedom or restlessness becomes too much for the other. It means looking at your life as a series of malleable choices, rather than as a set of train tracks with predictable stops.

*

Or, if it is a set of train tracks, it means thinking about who built the tracks and who made the timetable.

*

We drift back to ourselves, away from the hazy potential of other possibilities that wait in shadows just beyond our bravado.

*

Lisa Robertson has a phrase that fits the shadowy possibilities of friendship that I'm trying to articulate: *the dark body of friendship*. I want to pick up this phrase and unspool it, but let me give you its context first. Here's the larger set of ideas that Robertson is working with: *This word community is a common currency right now in poetry blogs and certain bars. Community's presence or absence, fail-*

ure, responsibility, supportiveness, etc.—everyone is hovering around this word. It could be that I just feel its ubiquity since I moved to rural France from Vancouver, ostensibly away from "my community." When I think about it from here I feel ambivalent. I don't miss community at all. I do miss my friends. How much of this notion of community is an abstraction of the real texture of friendship, with all its complicated drives and expressions—erotic, conversational, culinary, all the bodily cultures concentrated in a twisty relation between finite, failing persons. When I try to think of what a friend is, I imagine these activities we pleasurably share with someone we love—grooming, reading, sleeping, sex perhaps but not necessarily, intellectual argument, the exchange of books, garments and kitchen implements, all these exchanges and interweavings that slowly transform to become an idea and then a culture. Or a culture first, a culture of friends, and then an idea. Or both simultaneously. Writing is an extension and expression of friendship. Maybe friendship is more dangerous to think about and talk about because of its corporal erotics, mostly not institutionalized, not abstracted into an overarching concept and structure of collective protocols. For me, the drive to talk, to be in a room with someone I want to laugh or dance or fight with, to feed, all of those things—this has more to do with how writing happens for me, and also how I receive others' writing, than community does. I think my friends have become models and incentives for my relationships with books and writing. Certainly I primarily write to my friends and for them, seeking to please and delight them above all, and sometimes mysteriously and painfully fall-

ing out. But I don't want to call this community. I want to pre-serve the dark body of friendship.[8]

Robertson sets up a tension between community and friendship not so much as an oppositional relationship but as significantly different sets of ideas and modes of relating. Community, for Robertson, is *an abstraction* of her experience of friendship. Riffing on this, I read community as a vocabulary that is stripped of the intimacies—by which I mean closeness in all its forms—of individual relationships. Community, I think, is a way of talking about friendship in the general while gesturing towards the specific. Community is a necessarily coded language that, at its best, facilitates organizational and institutional structures in which intimacies can occur. At its worst, the language of community is, as Robertson suggests, abstraction without substance. Makers without materials; ideologies without individuals.

*

Friendship, for Robertson, is that more dangerous realm of experience. Friendship defies naming, she suggests, because it operates outside what Emmanuel Levinas (and others) have referred to as "the circle of the same"; it refuses to have its beautiful difference translated into something *I* understand on my own terms.

---

8. Lisa Robertson, "Dispatches from Jouhet!" *Harriet* n.d. <http://www.poetryfoundation.org/harriet/2009/11/lisa-robertson-dispatch-from-jouhet/>. [emphasis added]

Rosi Braidotti writes of it as a nomadic subjectivity; it's on the move, always, to escape being pinned down neatly with its wings spread.

Movement and female friendship are recurrent themes. Monique Wittig has written in *The Straight Mind* about lesbian identity being outside the lexicon of heteronormative language and culture. In saying *lesbians are not women*, Wittig underscores the heterosexual imperative of patriarchal culture as well as the ways in which categories like "woman" are socially constructed.[9] Her formulation refuses to participate in the oppressive naming practices of patriarchal culture. Perhaps friendship as such cannot be named because there exists no language for it in patriarchal discourse; it is quite literally outside language.

Elizabeth Grosz writes about architecture this way, which I love. For her, women are always outside of architecture, because buildings construct spaces for sanctioned bodies. *It is not that architecture excludes embodiment*, writes Grosz, *but what is not embodied is the idea of sexual difference.... Bodies are always absent in architecture, but they remain architecture's unspoken condition.*[10] Could we say the same of women's friendships? That they are outside of the architecture of popular discourse, but not absent from it? Outside, because

9. Monique Wittig, "One Is Not Born a Woman," *The Straight Mind: And Other Essays* (New York: Harvester/Wheatsheaf, 1980) 21–32.

10. Elizabeth Grosz, *Architecture from the Outside: Essays on Virtual and Real Space* (Boston: MIT Press, 2001) 13–14.

they subvert an *unspoken condition* of patriarchal culture; necessary, because their existences are an *unspoken condition* upon which that culture rests?

Maybe friendship is more dangerous to think about and talk about because of its corporal erotics, mostly not institutionalized, not abstracted into an overarching concept and structure of collective protocols.[11] The danger that Robertson points to has revolutionary potential. This potential is, to my mind, what she suggests by noting that corporeal erotics are inherent to friendships. There are bodies with other bodies—laughing, crying, cooking, dancing, hugging—with no imperative to procreation or other reproductive labours. Friendship as counter to capitalist ideology. Friendship as its own economy.

*

While Robertson doesn't suggest that she's talking specifically about friendship between women, I think her notion of the danger of thinking and talking about friendship is useful for considering female friendship. If thinking and talking about friendship (as opposed to....) is counter-institutional, then surely thinking and talking about female friendship is an absolute insurgency. Writing and talking about intimate same-sex friendships that fly in the face of persistent hetero-relational messaging, bearing witness to a friend's experience, and participating in an economy that's

---

11. If this looks familiar, it's because it's Lisa Robertson again.

outside normative narratives is heavy work. Vital, yes. And heavy. It is work that has no currency to mark its labour and its value.

★

My wariness around other women—my wariness around myself—lasted for longer that I would like to admit. I felt like there were competing narratives I didn't understand or have the tools to manage. I have too many stories of ferociously close friendships with women that, for one reason or another, fell apart. It was as though we would get too close, too dependent on one another, and one day, suddenly, the barometric pressure of the relationship would shift, and just like that, drift would happen. There are points in female friendship where the intimacy and witnessing become too much both for the world in which it exists and for the language of the world as it is.

★

I think, for example, of seeing a careful set of thin white scars on a new friend's arm, of saying nothing, but rolling up my own sleeve. I think of my friend knowing long before I did that a partner was cheating on me and waiting as much for me to catch up as to catch me when I was ready to see. I think of witnessing my friend—so many of my friends—recount in snatches of conversations, in undertones, in whispers, their experiences of gender-based violence. I think of the floodgate that opened *again* when

Emma Healey wrote "Stories Like Passwords" and of the backlash that followed.[12] I think of the way that some Brave Women On the Internet—El Jones, Stacey May Fowles, Anne Thériault, Rebecca Blakey, Scaachi Koul—speak truths that stop me in my tracks, and of how I struggle, ashamed at my inability to gather the right words to reply, or at least to say *I'm here, listening*.

Sometimes, when you've let another person see you directly in unfiltered light, it's you who walks away from them. I've had friends walk away after these moments of witness. I've been the friend who walks away. Sometimes, friendship falters and disappoints. Sometimes *I* falter and disappoint. That hurts. It still hurts.

*

Perhaps we can read another facet of Robertson's phrase, *the dark body of friendship*. Perhaps that darkness indicates not only the privacy and generative secrecy that can be conjured when operating at the margins of discourse. Maybe it also gestures towards what happens at the tangled intersections of lived realities. I can talk feminist killjoy theories and ideas all day, but when I leave my writing and return to the business of everyday life, I am living in a present that is saturated with misogyny. I am living in a present moment built on negative narratives about women and other others.

---

12. Emma Healey, "Stories Like Passwords," *The Hairpin* 6 Oct 2014 <https://thehairpin.com/stories-like-passwords-bf04e46c3fb6#.bwkhpaoly>.

Those narratives are, as Sara Ahmed writes, *sticky*.[13] They accrete. They build up. They weigh me down. The dark body of friendship might also indicate the heaviness of our trying and failing and trying again to care for each other.

I've read about female friendships described as romances and as the last bastion of truly platonic desire. This narrative appeals to me—it's resonant with Robertson's *dark body of friendship*—but it also makes me wary. It seems to me that recycling one storyline—the romance—means dragging all the sedimented associations of that storyline with you. I'm more interested in naming the ways this world does not make room for female friendship and discussing the ways those friendships form and thrive, despite the world as it is.

And working to build new worlds.

★

Remember, Ahmed says killing joy as a world-making project means killing the so-called joys of patriarchal culture. Reheated narratives of toxic women and catty girlfriends? No. Just no. There are better, truer stories to tell, and if we keep telling these better stories, then the world we want will be the world we're speaking, writing, and living.

★

---

13. Ahmed, *The Cultural Politics of Emotion* 11.

In "Friendship as a Way of Life," the late Michel Foucault was asked by his interviewer to think about gay desire. I don't know what the interviewer was expecting—I mean, it's Foucault, so come on—but Foucault responded with one of the most beautiful treatises on friendship I've ever encountered. Instead of thinking about desire as a primarily or solely sexual force, Foucault shifts its focus. Desire, he suggests, is a way of organizing your attentions and intentions. Desire between gay men, for Foucault, becomes a way to subvert the hegemony of compulsory heterosexuality. Desire, here, becomes openness to a range of intimacies that have been forbidden. Embraces. Nearness. Vulnerability. Desire for these things is, for Foucault, a desire for a new way of life.

*

What would female friendship as a way of life look like? As Foucault notes, in the history of Western culture, intimacies between women have been and are sanctioned and regulated in very different ways than they are and have been for men. Intimacies among women are expected at the same time as they are policed. Caregiving is almost unequivocally the domain of women, for example. And never mind the labour of caring for the body of another—more on that in another essay. Let's rest for a moment in the way that the intimacies of female friendship get refracted through a lens of caregiving.

*

Early in *The Politics of Friendship*, Jacques Derrida turns to
Aristotle as a way of thinking through friendship. Aristotle writes friendship, love, and death into the same equation, notes Derrida. For Aristotle, the essential question is
whether it is better to love or be loved; to know the other
or to be known by him. This triangulated calculus of intimacy—love / death / friendship—is, for Aristotle and Derrida
both, most easily worked out by turning to the relationship
between a mother and her child.

Actually, that's not quite right. The relationship that Aristotle refers to is one in which the mother places her child
in the care of a nurse, so it's the nurse who becomes the
child's primary caregiver, while the mother is once-removed
yet loves the child nonetheless. Derrida (through Aristotle) reads this as an example of the egoless possibilities of
friendship: the mother loves her child, while knowing that
the child doesn't have a clue who she is, nor does the child
love her back. The selfless love of the mother becomes the
foundation upon which the entirety of the argument is built.

*

But I see something different here. Putting to the side the
historical context for a moment, what *other* kind of intimate
friendship can we read onto this gendered example? What
if we read this not as the politics of friendship, but as the
politics of child care? Or the politics of women's labour?

Or the politics of a reproductive economy in which women who bear children are in financially stable situations that enable them to employ other women to care for those children, thus creating not a better but a more complex system of economic and intimate relationships? What if we read this as a prototype of the feminist utopia in *Herland*?[14] Or what if we read it as a gendered master–slave dialectic? My point here is that female friendships have a long history of functioning as metaphors for other things, rather than being read as the things in themselves. What would female friendship as a way of life look like?

*

If we look, there are myriad examples of female friendships that defy the limited narratives we typically see in mainstream media. Take, for example, the friendship between Mary McCarthy and Hannah Arendt. No one understood it, not really. As Michelle Dean writes, despite the fact that Arendt and McCarthy wrote to each other about topics as various as George Eliot, Cartesian dualism, Eldridge Cleaver, Kant, G. Gordon Liddy, and Sartre, their friendship was referred to by contemporaries and historians

---

14. *Herland* was written in 1915 by Charlotte Perkins Gilman. It's a novel about a group of women living in isolation together, reproducing asexually, and sharing child care and household labours. Lindy West has an awesome review/reimagining of a twenty-first-century version, which you can find here: <https://www.theguardian.com/lifeandstyle/2015/mar/30/herland-forgotten-feminist-classic-about-civilisation-without-men>.

as a romance (if it is mentioned at all).[15] Their friendship was reduced to the usual tropes: catty women gossiping together, ambitious women plotting together. When they were both panned in the same year—Arendt for *Eichmann in Jerusalem*, McCarthy for *The Group*—they supported each other through the critical storms. They were intellectual comrades. They had bumps and disagreements. They were not identical in their politics or their presentations of self. And they were immensely close, for decades.

*

Or how about Gail King and Oprah Winfrey, whose decades-long friendship is so incomprehensible that mainstream media continually frames it as a scandalous lesbian relationship?

Or Tina Fey and Amy Poehler?

I want to know more about what Nina Simone and Miriam Makeba talked about.

I would love to be invited to hear Sachiko Murakami and angela rawlings talk to each other about art and writing.

15. Michelle Dean, "The Formidable Friendship of Hannah Arendt and Mary McCarthy." *The New Yorker* 4 Jun 2013 <http://www.newyorker.com/books/page-turner/the-formidable-friendship-of-mary-mccarthy-and-hannah-arendt>.

I want to tell you that my friendship with C. transforms how I move through the world.

★

I want the generosity and an expansiveness of friendship as a way of life.

I want the worlds that may be possible if we take the feminist killjoy's multiple versions of friendship as a way of life.

★

I want to make friends with you here, on this page.

★

To write "I am a woman" is full of consequences.[16] Nicole Brossard wrote that, and many of her readers have taken it up as shorthand for addressing all of the ways that women's everyday experiences both exceed representation and are overwritten by available narratives.

---

16. Nicole Brossard, "To Write: In the Feminine Is Heavy with Consequences," *Fluid Arguments*, ed. Susan Rudy. Trans. Ann-Marie Wheeler (Toronto: Mercury, 2005) 110. Brossard wrote the phrase "I am a woman" in English, and the whole statement has been translated fully into both English and French. In a conversation with Susan Rudy, Brossard apparently told her that the claim made in English was meant to underscore not only gender but the complicated language politics of Franco- and Anglo-Canada.

Brossard writes *"Écrire 'je suis une femme' est plain de con-sequences."* Is it simply taking up space by identifying as a woman that is full of consequences? Is it to write "I am a woman" in English as a Francophone that is full of conse-quences? It is both and more. In just four words, Brossard asserts and demonstrates how taking up space by identify-ing as a woman—through a body of language—is full of consequences.

Ain't I a Woman?[17] Sojourner Truth wrote that, and I remem-ber reading it first in an undergraduate literature class taught by Professor Mae Henderson. *Listen to the rhetorical exper-tise in Truth's questioning,* she told us. We were encouraged to listen to Professor Henderson with our whole selves as she read Truth's words aloud. *Listen, because she would have spoken, rather than written, them first,* Professor Henderson urged us. *Listen to what kind of body-memory it would take to memorize and recite this, rather than read it. Imagine what kind of body of knowledges and experiences she would have had to live these truths and express them to us, across differences and distances and time.*

*

Two women. One white and Quebecoise, the other Black and a survivor of enslavement. Both brilliant questioners of the status quo. Both reach with words across abysses of

---

17. Truth first gave her speech in 1851. Read a version of it here: <http:// legacy.fordham.edu/ halsall/ mod/ sojtruth-woman.asp>.

difference and, without translating that difference, offer a space to meet and think.

*

This, too, is a kind of friendship, isn't it?

*

I come back to Brossard's statement and Truth's question as a place to settle my own thinking. I find that I do that a lot—return to things I've read before. I am a chronic re-reader. (Actually, I am a re-watcher, too. As my parents are fond of reminding me, there was a strange period in my childhood, in those first few months after we moved, when I watched and re-watched Bing Crosby and Rosemary Clooney dance around singing about the holidays...) I've been thinking about some of the books I've read and reread as I write and think here about friendship among women. I find myself coming back to preparing for my PhD candidacy exams as a moment when a penny dropped for me.

While studying for these exams, I had the luxury of reading scores of books by women writing in the twentieth and twenty-first centuries. One weekend, I read works by Toni Morrison and Zora Neale Hurston. I had been saving these books—*Sula*, *Their Eyes Were Watching God*—because I'd loved them so much when I read them in high school. Remember, I went to school in the southern United States, where racial politics were and are paramount, but circulate,

I think, in very different ways than in Canada, where racial politics were and are paramount, too. So the books I read for my English classes were by Toni Morrison, who had just published *Beloved* at the time and was on *Oprah*. My English class wrote a letter to Oprah, imploring her to let us be on the show with Morrison (no luck, alas). We also read *I Know Why the Caged Bird Sings* by Maya Angelou.

I loved them all, but as a teenager, I'd especially loved Hurston's *Their Eyes Were Watching God*. I loved Janey's perseverance. I mean, she *survived so fucking much*. But coming back to the book nearly a decade later, with an archive of feminist theory fresh in my mind, I found something different.

As I was reading the novel in Calgary, Alberta, I noticed that one of the things I'd liked so much about Janey was what I'd thought of as her self-reliance. Reading the book again, however, I realized that Janey's entire story—her first dismal marriage, her amazing romance with Tea Cake, her acquittal—wouldn't exist without her friend Phoeby.

This realization floored me.

Bookmark the fact that the publication history of the novel is complicated. Richard Wright and Ralph Ellison wrote scathing reviews of it, and other reviews damned it with faint praise or tied its worth to Hurston's gender. Flag for yourself how crucial Hurston's work and her life are and how few people know of it. Know that in part because her politics and aesthetics differed from the leading Black male writers of the day—not to mention her gender and her Blackness in a system of white supremacy—she and her writing fell into relative obscurity. She wrote more than fifty works of literature and journalism and was an accomplished anthropologist who conducted extensive field research. But until 1973, when Alice Walker went looking for and found Hurston's grave, it, and all her work, was largely forgotten. Say a fervent *thank you* to Alice Walker for marking Hurston's grave, publishing "In Search of Zora Neale Hurston" in 1975 in *Ms. Magazine,* and bringing Hurston and her oeuvre back into public discourse. Appreciate Walker's act of female friendship with another writer as a gesture of friendship that crosses generations and does not end at the death of one friend.

Move beyond the fact that Janey survived first emotional and then physical abuse. Put aside for the moment that her lover went rabid after being bitten by a dog and she had to shoot him to save her own life. Set aside the bizarre and significant fact that a bunch of white women show up as witnesses to Janey's defence and settle on this: the only reason any of us get to glimpse Janey's extraordinary life is because her best friend asked her how she was.

After returning home to Eatonville, where everyone is gossiping about her, Janey walks down the street in her overalls, her hair hanging loose down her back, and she heads straight over to Phoeby's house.

And what does Phoeby say?

How are you? Tell me what's been going on.

And Janey does. She sits on Phoeby's stoop and tells her everything. The good, the not-so-good, the really-bloody-awful, Janey tells her friend all of it. And then they laugh. Janey mends the last parts of her that need mending by talking to her friend Phoeby, who listens, who asks the right questions, and who lets her friend talk.

*

Together, on Phoeby's stoop, they make a world.

Chapter 3:
Notes on Feminist Mothering

I am sitting at the kitchen table, sweating in my socks. It's 5:50 a.m. I've been looking at my computer screen for nearly an hour. I am getting over a cold—the kind of cold that leaves you shaken even after the acute symptoms have dissipated. *I am not well!* I have wanted to lie on the floor and whisper that until someone, preferably in clean hospital scrubs, comes to pick me up and put me into bed. I have wanted the coolness of sheets. The coolness of a hand on my forehead.

When I was small and I got sick, my mother would stay home with me. She would set me up in my bed with ginger ale and a book, if I was feeling well enough. Usually, though, I wouldn't stay home until I was at the point of sickness that feels like you're in an altered state of reality. My mother would come in and flip my pillow to the cool side, or bring me an ice cube tied in a handkerchief to suck on, which would slow my bronchial hacking. And me, I'd lie there in bed, floating, cared for.

Now, as an adult, there's not much being cared for that happens when I'm sick. Not for any of us, I don't imagine, though frankly I tend not to be expansive and generous in my thinking when I'm sick, and that's what I am today. Sick. Where is my cool hand? Where is my mom? Who is going to hold me up and patiently bring me ginger ale as though it's the only thing that matters to them in their day? It's narcissism to say that when I get sick I feel like I am *really* sick. The sickest (as if it were a competition). But isn't that what Freud says about narcissists? That the invalid is the most perfect example, for she can only turn inwards, towards herself, towards the ailment. So maybe it makes sense that I think about being cared for when I'm sick. Anyway, when I was small and sick, I would lie in bed in a haze and every now and then my mother would come and check my temperature, give me ginger ale, lay a hand on my forehead, and I felt held.

Now, my role has shifted. Now, I do the holding.

Now I am a mother, and I am sick, and I am sitting at my kitchen table trying to write. Don't feel sorry for me; I chose most of this. Later (hours later, I hope), I will hear my daughter start to sing in her crib. She's not quite a year old, yet, so indulge me when I say *sing*. She will say *Bah!* and *Mamamama!* and *Da!da!da!* There will be some raspberries blown. In recent mornings, when I've gone into her room to get her from her crib, she's sitting up with her stuffed animals gathered around her, a small, plush chorus, ready to back her up on the *bah bah bahs*. Even more recently, she's there, standing in her strange sleeping bag with arm holes, holding onto the railing of her crib. She smiles when I come in, my girl does. Not immediately, not always. Some days, for a few seconds, she regards me solemnly. Having not spent any time around babies until I had my own, I was not versed in the solemnity of infants. It's a thing to behold. In those moments I understand my friend's partner, who has been overheard to say that his baby seems to look into his soul. I have no time for this kind of self-indulgence in any other part of the day, but so help me, in the morning when I am not yet coffeed and not yet girded in cynicism, I am taken off guard when my daughter appraises me, standing there, blinking her huge, serious eyes at me. *Ah yes, you*, I imagine she thinks, *Hello. Are you up to the task today?* And for a second I stand there, looking back, thinking, *Am I?* And then she smiles, and it is a ridiculous mouthful-of-new-baby-teeth smile. It encompasses her whole body. She wriggles with delight. And with that, the spell is broken—or recast—and we get down to the business of bodily care and everyday life.

*

Mothering. Being a mother. I am a mother. That's a harder category and concept for me to think through than *feminist*; it's easier for me to understand and say *I am a feminist* than *I am a mother*. I've been trying to think about why that is, and I have come to this: I've studied feminist thought and theory in academic settings, and while some of the texts I've studied have addressed mothering—even feminist mothering—the academy is not a space that makes room for childbearing or child care or parenting. I've watched my mentors struggle with work–life balance. I've watched peers and colleagues fall behind, get passed over, or work themselves sick to manage a research and teaching career without letting the fact of their children get in the way. I have internalized all of this. And so, when my partner and I decided to try and have a child, I found that my most immediate challenge was my own internalized conception of what this oceanic shift would mean for *me*. I found the language for fretting about work, about my own research, about how—and whether—I'd be seen once I had a baby.

*

I remember reading Doris Lessing's *The Golden Notebook* about a decade ago. The novel is set in England and spans the 1930s–50s. Anna Wulf is the protagonist, and the Golden Notebook is the culmination of four other notebooks in which Anna has been recording her life. She's a member of the Communist Party. She's divorced. She has a best friend, Molly, with whom she often has strained and tense periods. They are both trying to carve out spaces for themselves in an ostensibly radical milieu that, as it turns out (surprise!) is in fact patriarchal and oppressive. Anna and Molly fret about politics, their place in the Party, their children, and their work. Because all of the notebooks are Anna's, we're privy to her battles—with motherhood, with making space for her own work, and in her attempts to be a Free Woman. We see her struggle, and that struggle is raw. The contradictions—of possibility, of reality—are staggering. Anna unravels. This novel got under my skin and stayed there. I find myself thinking about it more, recently. I think about how Anna *looks* like a Thoroughly Modern Woman and how she *feels* pulled to bits by the demands (material, emotional) on her.

*

Not thirty seconds after she left my body, my new daughter was opening her tiny bird mouth and looking for my nipple. Rooting. It's called rooting. I thought of pigs in muck. Smart animals, pigs. The midwife was thrilled. The nurse patted me on the shoulder. My partner narrated what was going on for me because I was so tired I couldn't see and, frankly, couldn't muster more than a moment of wonder—less awe, more self-satisfaction in a job done. My girl was still attached to her umbilical cord when she latched. I had never felt less in my own body than at that moment.

I mean this: I felt like I was falling. And falling and falling and falling. I didn't have vertigo, *per se*, nor an out-of-body experience. I just felt outside of myself. There was our daughter who, until moments ago, was inside of me. A small, gender-neutral Matryoshka doll, nested inside my enormous womb. Until moments before we'd referred to her as FM—Fetus Maximus—refusing to tie her too soon to the weight of categorization. FM was there, but not-there. I was not-me, but I was still me. A bigger, less-of-a-night-owl me, granted, but still me. And then FM was our daughter. And I was me, but I was also mom. In that moment I felt the epistemological shift profoundly. I didn't recognize myself, and I didn't feel at home. I became aware of my animal status. There, with an infant on my breast, with my partner, with the midwife sewing me back together and the nurse checking equipment and the surgeon expressing surprise, I felt vulnerable and foreign and strange. Even (especially?) with the proof of my own so-called "normalcy" (hospital speak for a vaginal birth, for uncomplicated breastfeeding, for an infant who passes the Apgar test). I felt uncanny.

*

Is uncanny the right word? I remember writing a paper in graduate school on Freud's theory of the uncanny and being surprised to find where the term and the idea came from. It's from Hoffmann's *Der Sandmann*. Poor Nathanael, the main character, falls in love with Olimpia, who, as it turns out, is not a real girl, but an automaton. Lots of things happen in this horror show of a short story, but Freud gets stuck on Nathanael's mistake about Olimpia: she is uncanny. Not real, but not not real. Bumping up against his mistake and looking at it in the eye (her eyes!) makes Nathanael tumble away from sanity. For Freud, the uncanny involves a fear of having your own eyes taken from you—a kind of ocular sleight of hand signifying castration. So when Nathanael looks Olimpia the-not-real-girl in the not-real-eyes, he falls. And he falls and falls. And that—the falling—is what the uncanny is. The uncanny, a.k.a., the unheimlich—the unhomelike—is familiarity couched in weirdness. Something you know by heart but, upon second glance, that something is just *off*. It is familiar and *un-*. And so, when you return to the thing you know by heart, be it yourself, or your lover, or your home, and it is just so, just as you left it, it doesn't matter. But when it isn't "just so"… In the incongruity of the uncanny, what was is laid bare in its weirdness in the present. What's left to do but fall into it?

Maggie Nelson describes the complicated algebra of caring for yourself and for another as an ethics.[1] She's talking about birth, too, and falling is a recurrent theme. Nelson starts considering falling when she returns to D.W. Winnicott, whose observations about mothering she finds compelling. (Me too, but only when Nelson puts them into her own words.) Winnicott has this idea about the *good enough mother*. The good enough mother/primary caregiver is just that: good enough. This matters, because anyone could theoretically provide a good enough holding environment—one in which the child gets its needs met such that it doesn't remember— doesn't *have* to remember—any bump in its babyhood. That is to say that there are bumps, to be sure, but those bumps aren't so devastating as to need to be remembered as a means of self-protection.

(I tell myself this while a slow cut of my girl hurling her-

1. Maggie Nelson, *The Argonauts* (Minneapolis: Graywolf Press, 2015) 33.

self off a bed onto the floor is on technicolour replay in my mind...)

But the crux for Winnicott seems to be, at least in part, that the mother lives her own erasure. She exists in the uncanny crucible of herself becoming m/other. The real point is that the child is cared for *well enough*. Yet, if the child is not provided with a good enough holding environment (for whatever reason), the results can be severe. Nelson describes it this way:

Falling for ever

All kinds of disintegration

Things that disunite the psyche and the body

Going to pieces

Falling for ever

Dying and dying and dying

Losing all vestige of hope of the renewal of contacts[2]

The irony in Winnicott's formulation is this: If the child's holding environment is good, then she won't remember it. It will flow together seamlessly and become a kind of

---

2. Ibid.

taken-for-granted care environment. The primary caregiver (often the mother) is the only one who will remember that quotidian duty of care. That's the erasure I'm striving for: for my girl to forget everything I do in the small and daily hours. I am striving for her to be well-held, and in that holding, I ensure an erasure of myself.

*

That's complicated. I admit it, I feel complicated about not being remembered. I find myself thinking, again, about that Aristotelian geometry of friendship in which love for another happens without the promise of reciprocation. It is hard, this daily practice of loving fiercely and showing it in banal and vital ways. Nursing, for example: months of nights pinching myself to stay awake while the small creature was nourished by me. She won't remember my bleary exhaustion, my sore body, and thank goodness for that. That's the erasure I am striving for.

*

I realize I do not remember being held in all those small moments as an infant.

That means I was well held.

That means I've forgotten, mom. I see that now.

*

There is a difference between *mothering* and *parenting*. Several. There are several differences. I find myself trying to think through these differences, as my partner and I learn how to share the work of caring for bébé, make space for our own work, our own care, and care for each other. I find myself thinking through these differences, as our little family shifts from being emergent (and in a state where emergency doesn't feel far off) to evolving, no longer unfamiliar in this new configuration of togetherness. Moving forward, constantly becoming, but without the kind of raw franticness of a newborn with two new parents.

Parenting makes room, I think. It is an expansive term. It queers the heteronormativity of man + woman = baby = family. Thank goodness. *Parenting* also makes room for, well, parents. It sounds obvious, but on a structural level, it makes room for people who do not give birth to take parental leave and gives weight to the responsibility for children *in public*. *Mothering* has different connotations. For one thing, it is a deeply gendered term and is coded as a private relation. It is feminized labour, mothering. I want the two terms to be co-equal. This feels silly to write, frankly, but I do. I want *parent* and *mom* to signal the same kinds of things. But they don't. They just don't. And there's a kind of damage in that difference: I read as *mom* because of my age (37), my cisgender, and the fact that I was able to grow a fetus and give birth to a baby. Being called *the mom next door* by my younger female neighbour is both a privilege of recognition—I *am* a mom next door!—and an erasure—it wasn't meant to be flattering; rather it flattened me into a typecast role.

And what if I was the trans-mom next door?

Or the mom of colour?

Or the differently abled mom?

There's more to the cultural weight of *mother* versus *parent* than simply supplanting one word with another. There are nuances and specificities of experience that get lost. And there's a complexity of affective attachments that get smoothed over with these words, too.

*

Recently, a friend sent me Rufi Thorpe's "Mother, Writer, Monster, Maid."[3] Exploring the myriad contradictions between the mundane beauty of mothering small children, heterosexual partnership, and creative work (she's a writer), Thorpe really drills into her own identification as mother, writer, and partner. Labour and visibility are at the heart of her inquiry. Here are a few lines my friend highlighted:

"Sometimes," I said to my mother the other day, "I feel they will devour me. I feel they will use me up like a tube of toothpaste and

3. Rufi Thorpe, "Mother, Writer, Monster, Maid," *Vela: Written By Women* n.d. <http://velamag.com/mother-writer-monster-maid/>.

never even notice." She nodded, watching me cry in her living room, my baby crawling on her floor.

"They will," she said.

For Thorpe, the cultural sedimentation of expectations of mothering are not straightforward. Instead, there are small and often vague ways in which her labour—both emotional and material—are at once vital and invisible:

I often feel that the work I do around the house is the work of an invisible person. How else could my husband consistently leave his underwear tucked behind the bathroom door? His wet towel on the bed? Surely, he does not imagine me, swearing, swooping to pick up his damp, crumpled briefs with a child on one hip as I listen to a podcast and ponder going gluten free. He is not making a statement with his actions, saying, "Here, wife, pick up after me." Instead, I think that on some level he believes that he lives in an enchanted castle where the broom comes to life and sweeps, and the teapot pours itself.

It hurts to read that passage. It hurts because of the ways I recognize myself in what she writes and because of how I don't want to recognize myself, not there. The piece that plucks at my heart the most is that image of Thorpe swearing, bending down, picking up, and cleaning, while carrying a toddler. I did that this morning, while wondering if I am too focused on tidiness and worrying that I am not often very much fun.

Who or what makes me think that?

I know that this invisibilizing of labour is not the purview of heterosexual relationships alone. It's those markers of heterosexuality in Thorpe's description—signifiers like "husband" and "wife"—that depict so plainly the patriarchal narrative of how *mothering* differs from *parenting*. Yes, there is something profound and singular for each body that bears a being in it and births it into the world. No doubt. But what I want to trouble as a feminist killjoy is that particular narrative of *mother* that makes labour invisible and oppressive. As a feminist killjoy I am working to both name and refuse that narrative that calls me *the mom next door* but will not call my partner *the dad next door*. What would it look like if we (all of us) refused the derogative, the banal, the boring, the invisible, the abject, and the long-suffering as de facto *mother*?

*

In a section of *The Argonauts* where she's reaching for language to name her own life, her own desires, her own queer family, Nelson employs a kind of negative dialectics. Rather than pin it down, where the "it" is actually an assemblage of affective and material forces—birth, caregiving, fucking, family-making, queerness, work, writing—she turns to critical theory to say what it is not. Not Lacan's Real/Symbolic. Not Freud's Oedipal extravaganza. Not Rancière's event. Not Žižek's crisis ordinary. Not totem. Not taboo. Not heteronormative. Not without privilege, but with the recognition that not even privilege can entirely ward off suffering. Not singular. Not static. Not nameable. Not confined to one descriptor or pronoun.

But what if falling is a falling away, a sort of loosening of the armature of not-ness? Out of that armature we might emerge, different, unexpected, shaking our new selves with the unsteady and marvellous promise of a colt standing for the first time. And what if the contracts of human relations we hope to have renewed are not the ones that treat us well? What if it isn't such a great or generative thing to be bound to convention? In other words, what if the answers are not singular? Are not single? What if they are significant and perspective-altering events and we let them be? In other words, what if contradictions and evolutions in how we live as families are just that: dynamic trajectories that are ever-evolving. I think that that's where Nelson lands, however briefly. I want to land there longer. The answers—how should a person be, what makes a family, what is a good enough "mother"—are not single or static. What if multiplicities became the place from which mainstream discourses about mothering start?

And what if falling is just too freighted a word? After all, wasn't it Anne Carson who eschewed falling in favour of suggesting that we might *aeroplane* into love?[4] I like that image: you and an other hurtling through the air in a tin can, wondering *is this a good idea?* Knowing it doesn't matter because you're in it until the ride is done.

---

4. Anne Carson, "Short Talk on the Sensation of Airplane Takeoff," *Short Talks* (London, ON: Brick Books, 1992) 42.

*

It occurs to me that mothering is a bit like aeroplaning: propelled into something seemingly extra-human (outside the self), yet here we are, human and along for the ride.

*

And perhaps feminism is a bit like walking purposefully through a crowd.

*

I thought these things while pushing my daughter in a stroller down Las Ramblas in Barcelona. The two of us moving through a crowd together, uncertain of just where we were going and just as certain that no one would decide but us. I'm making this up, of course. Who knows what the infant was thinking. But I was thinking about us two, walking. About how the world looks at me differently when I'm pushing a stroller. Women—and some men, but mostly women—make eye contact, sometimes. They tend to be pushing strollers, too. Younger women either coo or cut a wide berth away from me. I don't blame them; until I had E., didn't I, too, fall into that camp of baby-disinterest? There's that word again, *fall*. Young men are often the politest. This surprises me. My own surprise surprises me.

*

Before our daughter was born, I didn't have the language for thinking or talking about mothering. Kind of like how I didn't have a language for friendship among women, really. What does that mean? And what should I make of the fact that I have come searching for the two languages at the same time?

What I did have was a great big abyss of unknowing. And a collection of observations and anecdotes—often contradictory—about how mothers are valued. And here's what I can say: I feel ambivalent at best about what I see. Now that I'm looking, especially in the places I spend the most time (university campuses), I see the absences: rarely are children there. There are looks of surprise, delight, and, albeit infrequently, disdain when my partner or I take our daughter to campus, which we do often on account of our schedules, lack of family close by, need to work, and lack of regular child care. My partner, B., started a new contract two months after our daughter was born. I took a full load of sessional teaching in September. Bébé was three months' old. Often, B. and I would meet in the office of the English Department's head administrator. The wonderful M.B. would hold our girl as we swapped her diaper bag and carrier. On Tuesdays, I would bring the baby to campus to meet C., who is finishing her PhD and has a child of her own in daycare. C. would take the baby for four or five hours while I wildly prepped for a three-hour night class and B. finished an enormous teaching day. So hear me when I say the girl has spent a great deal of time on a campus. And hear me also when I say that I can think of only one other baby I've ever seen on a university campus. That's bizarre, isn't it?

Or maybe it's not bizarre. Maybe what's odd is that *feminist* and *mother* still rest uneasily with one another. Not allies so much as chafing positions. Multiplicity and contradiction as perception-altering. As events that make mothers.

When Nelson works through her own archive of references to childbearing and mothering, she comes up short, too. Or rather, while the women are working—as academics, as radicals, as punks—the children are there.

...generally speaking, even in the most radical feminist and/or lesbian separatist circles, there have always been children around (Cherríe Moraga, Audre Lorde, Adrienne Rich, Karen Finley, Pussy Riot... the list could go on and on).[5]

I could make my own list, and I might. But what I am looking for right now is a better understanding of the schism between the theory and praxis of feminist mothering. As my friend J. says, *there's a disconnect between ideas and action or something. Also always the pushing against the maternal as total, while simultaneously trying to write about its totalizing affect... I dunno. I've had a really hard time with it.* Yes, that's it: the unsayable yet visceral experience of being myself and yet wholly and uncannily Other. The difficulty of trying to articulate the banal frustration upon realizing (again

---

5. Nelson 75.

and again, like a dull hammer on the heart) that mothering and child care are feminized labour. That they are feminized labour is not new. That there are still uphill battles that are being waged in my mind, on my body, and on the sidewalks of cities and the hallways of workplaces is not new. That I can write this and add my tiny document to the vast archives of poetry, theory, psychology, and sociological writing, not to mention mommy blogs, and *still* feel uncanny and uneasy with those parts of me (mom, feminist) is not new.

Sure, I've had incredible role models in friends, colleagues, writers and public figures who are fiercely feminist mothers. And yes, there absolutely are legions of men—queer, trans, and cis—who father fiercely. But let's not pretend that the gendered expectations of child caregiving don't differ. My focus here is on women and women-identified people. The position from which I live and write is this: I am cis-gendered. I am able-bodied. Though I was medically geriatric when I got pregnant, I was able to get pregnant without medical assistance, and I had a pretty uncomplicated pregnancy. I am white, and so is my partner. I have a male partner. Sperm was free, and the sex was fun. In short, I'm thinking about mothering and feminism from a position of real privilege.

*

Sarah Ahmed's notion of "sweaty concepts" undergirds my thinking here about feminism and mothering. For Ahmed, sweaty concepts is a way of demonstrating how the work of description and exploration is labour:

A concept is worldly but it is also a reorientation to a world, a way of turning things around, a different slant on the same thing. More specifically a "sweaty concept" is one that comes out of a description of a body that is not at home in the world. By this I mean description as angle or point of view: a description of how it feels not to be at home in the world, or a description of the world from the point of view of not being at home in it.... When I use the concept of "sweaty concepts" I am also trying to say we can generate new understandings by describing the difficulty of inhabiting a body that is not at home in a world. Sweat is bodily; we might sweat more during more strenuous activity. A "sweaty concept" might be one that comes out of a bodily experience that is difficult, one that is "trying," and where the aim is to keep exploring and exposing this difficulty, which means also aiming not to eliminate the effort or labour from the writing (I suspect not eliminating the effort or labour becomes an academic aim because we have been taught to tidy our texts, not to reveal the struggle we have in getting somewhere).[6]

When I went into labour, I was unprepared for how *hard* it was. I know, that's a ridiculous thing to write. Those of you who have been in labour are laughing right now. Yes, Erin, it is hard. Those of you who have not been in labour are also laughing, like, yeah, obviously it is hard. And I was

6. Sara Ahmed, "Sweaty Concepts," *feministkilljoys* 22 Feb 2014 <http://feministkilljoys.com/2014/02/22/sweaty-concepts/>.

not entirely naïve: I'd read about labour (though I'd not, as some folks I know, watched any videos on *YouTube*. You couldn't pay me enough). I'd read about pain, too. In fact, I had read somewhere that gallbladder pain rated higher on a pain scale than labour, and frankly, I'd felt smug. After all, I'd had my gallbladder out after years of chronic attacks. Surely I was some sort of pain master, right?

Not so much.

Labour was so hard that everything I'd planned went out the window. (Okay, not everything, because my birth plan was *don't die* and *have an alive baby*, but still. My partner and I had spent months mocking birth tanks—with due respect, water birth fans, all the photos of families in scummy tubs I found pretty hilarious—and then, boom, where do I spend hours whimpering incomprehensibly? Yup. Bathtub. Oh, the Alanis-Morrissette-style irony...) I moaned. I shook. I did not care one iota about all the things I thought I would care about (i.e., a zillion people prodding at my body in all its planet-sized vulnerability). At one point I projectile vomited on my partner, the nurse, and the midwife simultaneously. And they were not standing next to one another. So yeah, my understanding of the concept of labour and pain shifted pretty substantially over a twenty-four-hour period.

I like this idea that a concept is *worldly but... also a reorientation to a world*. Wresting my own understanding of "being a mother" into the ways in which I already understand myself is a sweaty concept. An actual reorientation to a world that is both familiar and strange. Who was it that put that post-modern slash in the word *m/other*? Julia Kristeva, I think.[7] She's the one who suggests that in the process of becoming our own individual selves, we have to cast off the mother to constitute our own identities in the world. M/other—other than, different. Uncanny. Familiar and strange. The thing we want and the thing we feel foolish for wanting. The person who by definition makes us children when what we think we want to be is adult, standing on our own two wobbly feet.

But that's my academic training at work, not my bodily experience. Not even, necessarily, my lived experience. And yet, all these things push against each other. And there's me, trying to figure out who I am in the midst of it. In the midst of my body and its oceanic shifts. That's me, in the midst of sweaty thinking, grappling with sweaty concepts.

*

Why is it so hard for me to write about being a mom and so easy for me to write about rape culture? Or, not so much easy as it is imperative. I can't stop writing when I sit down to address an aspect of rape culture. Yet, when I think through how I might wrestle with writing about feminism

---

7. Okay, it is Kristeva and Jacques Lacan and a whole host of critical theorists trained in psychoanalysis who build on or diverge from the way that Freud framed the mother in his triangulation of the modern family. Does this theoretical history of thinking through "mothers" really matter? Sort of, I think, depending on where you sit, because stories circulate and become myth or organizing principle, and Freud's story about how mothers work is a big one.

and mothering, I often feel stuck. I feel as though I don't have enough experience, but what does that even mean? I have a mother. I know mothers. And yet I so rarely talk about mothering.

*

Have I even taken a moment to mention how in love with this kid I am? I am utterly, completely, unexpectedly in love with this small, toddling, dog-loving, in-key-warbling little human.

*

Again, I think of how mothering might be a bit like aeroplaning. Only this time mothering is aeroplaning into every other hard thing I have taught myself to say. And the aeroplane is cotton and steel. Canny and un-. Homey, and not. What do you make of that?

*

Before my daughter was born, when I was pregnant enough not to be confusing, people started giving me advice. My partner got advice too, but not the same kind and not always from the same people. The advice that he received was more along the lines of how substantially our relationship would change. The advice I received fell into one of three camps that I have come to think of as the "Now That You're About to be a Mom, We Can Share Secrets" camp, the "Now That

You're About to be a Mom, You Should Know Your Life Is Over" camp, and "The Beauty of Motherhood Makes It All Worth It, You're a Goddess-Martyr" camp.

The Secrets camp advisors gave me advice the way you might pass a note in high school—furtive, confident that what you've written will change everything. And it did. They gave me advice like *get bendy straws if you breastfeed. You'll be so thirsty and stuck under a heavy lump of sleeping infant.* Or *prepare yourself for the freakshow that will be your own breasts.* Or *soak and freeze maxi pads. Seriously, just do it.* I filed these secrets away and used many of them. In those first emotionally and physically raw days and weeks post-birth, I devoured this information. It came, sometimes, from the most unexpected of people. Colleagues I only knew in a professional capacity sent me epistolary emails. Acquaintances I'd never spoken with in anything other than a hey-how's-the-weather capacity shared vulnerable stories with me about how to ease postpartum pain. A dear friend stole my heart when, over dinner early in our new friendship, she told me that the thing that scared her the most after giving birth was the anticipation of taking a shit again. I mean, really, why was no one telling me this in a public-health context?

The Life Is Over campers were less subtle. They tended to make pronouncements to my partner and me (not usually at the same time), and those pronouncements were about how I would become frigid and he would become frustrated. Or about how we would never sleep or eat or have conversations again. Or about how we were now on the short, steep slide into dinner at five and bed by seven and No Fun Ever Again. Or how I would never be at home in my body again, how I'd age and slide and sag in ways that weren't appropriate, but were inevitable. These pronouncements couched in advice-giving were offered to me by women, mostly, and it was offered with a kind of heavy shrillness, while it was men who most commonly offered these pronouncements to my partner. I shrunk from the Life Is Over campers, trying to shut out their advice while simultaneously grappling with how to process this information. Because much of it was coming from people I knew and trusted.

The Goddess-Martyrs were well meaning. I suppose everyone was well meaning in their own way, but the Goddess-Martyrs were *really* well meaning. They were the ones—again, men and women—who would tell me about the dark days and then remind me of the beautiful miracle that would be my child. As though bébé was a metonym for my pre-mother self. Feeling bad about your body? Look at that baby you made! Feeling disconnected from your own interests? Look at that baby you made! Feeling isolated/frustrated/tired/lonely/at your wit's end? LOOK AT THAT BABY YOU MADE AND BOW DOWN BEFORE HER SQUISHY CHEEKS! The takeaway point for me from these campers was that no feeling I had was more authentic than the miracle of birth. And while my partner assures me that it *was* a thing to behold, me pushing out bébé after one very long fucking day, I just can't accept that one miraculous thing trumps another. My sense of self, traded for our daughter's existence? I just don't buy that narrative whole-sale. I can't.

*

Are you reading this and shaking your head? I am too, sort of. I mean, it's so cliché, those second two camps of well-meaning advice-givers. And besides, who would take any of that advice to heart, uncritically?

Well, me, as it turns out. Especially the stuff from the Life Is Over campers. I've been thinking about why that is, and I realize that these narratives are deeply patriarchal in their bent and content. They adhere to the feminization of child care labour. They cling to the narrative of the divisiveness of children.

Despite all the progress made by radical feminism—raising consciousness around the gendered nature of domestic labour, for example—the overarching narratives of momming include keywords like guilt, shame, isolation, and loneliness. I was reaching for the words to say why I think this might be, and I couldn't find them. Or rather, as my friend S. says, I couldn't get out of my own way to say them. So I did what I often do. I asked the Internet. Here are what some of my friends, who are also mothers, had to say in response to my question: *Why is writing about momming while being a feminist so hard?*

J.: *Cuz you think about the future that will always need feminism.*

And remember this one, from a different J.? She wrote: *I feel like there's a disconnect between theory and praxis or something. Also always the pushing against the maternal as total, while simultaneously trying to write about its totalizing affect... I dunno. I've had a really hard time with it.*

N.: *Because you are caught in a conundrum of wanting to be positive (after all your child may read what you say) and address difficulties that are so personal it feels like a betrayal of partners and babies to address—because complaining while moment is hard because moment is full of conflict and intensity and boredom—frustration and gratitude—a profound sense of isolation and privilege?*

N. again: *Momming keeps getting rewritten as moment—which is a painful acknowledgment of mortality and the finite childhood you share—the short intimacy of mother–child—the deep bonding you are doing now that only you will remember and because when you write about something you open yourself up for argument and the moms are policed so much opening that door feels dangerous and stupid—(what if someone I respect thinks I am a bad mother!!!!)*

T.: *Because living in the world is hard while feminist. The only thing that's harder is living in the world while not feminist.*

K.: *All of the above. Plus, the immense power we have over these children. The sense in which under all the pressure that there is*

I'm failing daily in treating that power with utmost care. It's a deep deep nag. About which I don't want to write or talk, with anyone, really; and so it becomes a troubling secret. Because if I write or talk it plays so much into idealized sacrificial motherhood & policing of mothers & struggle of being confident while female.

S.: *Because mothers can't be people or we will harm the babies? Think of the babies!*

A different K.: *'Cause of all the apologies and guilt?*

N., who has lots of wise things to say: *Because women all over the world have it harder than me. Because the stakes are so high. Because am I doing a good enough job for my son? Because lots of women who don't want children end up taking care of elderly parents and other family at cost to their independence because as a society we don't recognize that their lives are also overwhelming. Because Boko Haram exists. Because we can't just throw out even the worst of men when they are our sons or brothers or fathers. Because feminism is complicated by race and class. Because Alice Walker is hated by her daughter. Because feminism is a position and a way of being not a cure-all, not a protective coating for my babies?*

And, oh gosh, this one got me: *Because both feminists and mothers can be really rough on each other and it is a special kind of awful pain to fight about things that matter so much to all of you.*

*

The hard part of this uncanny shift from me to mom-me is the way that women treat me.

*

The harder part of this uncanny shift is wondering how I have treated other mothers.

*

And then, I guess, I also have to reckon with how my own feminism comes home to roost. Am I kind and expansive in my theorizing of my own moods? Or do I fall into self-flagellation that looks pretty much like the patriarchal cultural norms I've been interpellated into?

A little from column "A," a little from column "B," so help me. Okay, often a lot from column "B."

*

Having a body that can (and does) give birth, and doing work. Those seem to be two things that set apart cultural narratives of mothering from cultural understandings of parenting. Talk around bodies is, I think, the most obvious. How your child-bearing body is pre-, during-, and post-bébé takes up so much psychic and discursive space. Medical professionals weigh in on it. Magazines weigh in on it. Strangers weigh in on it. Sure, there are cultural discourses around male-presenting bodies too, but they scan differently.

Remember how Leonardo DiCaprio highlighted again that aging as a man is acceptable and fashionable? *Dad-body* isn't a bad thing. You know what is? *Mom jeans*.

Work, though. Work and mothering seem even more difficult to reconcile. It's not just finding the time to work, or being okay with not working (as though caregiving isn't work...); it's the making invisible of labour that Thorpe talks about and that seems to saturate the subject position of being a mother.

As I got closer and closer to our baby's due date this spring, friends and colleagues offered other kinds of gentle advice. Not so much body or self or relationship advice. This time it was advice regarding my work. Take a break, they suggested. Don't put too much pressure on yourself. Decide to take a break from the blogging, from chairing the board of Canadian Women in the Literary Arts. Don't expect yourself to write or do much of anything else. Just be. Just learn how to be a family. And so, we did. My partner and I spent the summer months hanging out with the baby. Some days were hard, some days were not. Those first weeks were surreal—the longest days and the shortest weeks. And I spent a lot of time sitting, learning how to feed our girl. I read a lot of novels. I watched Netflix. A *lot*. I stared into space.

I did not spend any time thinking critically.

*

What do I even mean by that?

*

I mean I was me, but I was not me.

Perhaps that's not a surprise to you, but it was to me. I didn't expect the kind of hormonal hum that genuinely affected how my brain worked. And you know what? For the most part, that wasn't a big deal. I missed the critical thinking, but not that much. Not at first. But eventually, as we started to find our familial rhythm, as my body healed and our girl became more aware, more infant than newborn, as the autumn crept closer, I began to wonder what *would* move me back into active and deliberate critical thought. Anything? Nothing?

As it turned out, a last-minute emergency sessional hire moved me back into that space more quickly than we'd expected. And suddenly, after the first week of classes, after our household finished our collective first week of teaching + juggling bébé care, I was in an airplane on my way to Winnipeg for two-and-a-half days of "thinking critically" at a conference.

We'd planned for this, my partner and I. When I submitted my paper proposal, I was pregnant. We knew that as the date approached, we'd have to reassess what my travelling would mean for us both, as a new family with an infant. Ultimately we decided it was worth the added challenges.

After all, this would be the new normal, right? And I'd still want to think and write, wouldn't I? Of course I would.

And so, on a Thursday of the first week of classes, I hopped on a plane and flew west. I said goodbye to my partner and our baby, and I got on the plane. I packed my breast pump, theory books, and laptop in my carry-on. And I got on the plane.

I want to tell you that I cried. I want to tell you, on the other hand, that I didn't cry. That I was *thrilled* to have two-and-a-half days entirely to myself. The reality is that I did neither. Or rather, everything I did was so clouded by managing my breasts that I didn't really fall into anxiousness or ecstasy. I mostly just thought, listened, took notes, and, as soon as a session was over, slipped into the public washroom to pump.

It was odd.

But let me back up.

I arrived in Winnipeg at one in the morning, fell into a cab, got to where I was staying, and slept fitfully. A few hours later, I got myself to the conference at nine in the morning, ready to hear Lauren Berlant give her keynote address.

Oh yeah, did I mention that this was a conference on affect?

As I sat in the audience listening to Berlant theorize a poetics of dissociativeness, I felt what she was describing in my body. Dissociativeness, she posited, is something we do every day. According to Berlant, teaching is an experience of dissociative behaviour: we lecture while thinking about our next move and watching the student who is texting and the student who looks like she may be about to speak in the same moment that we feel our hearts race and wonder if our deodorant is holding up.

In that moment, I really got it. I mean I understood what she was saying in a visceral way. I realized, as I sat in a washroom expressing milk so that I could continue to feed my girl when I got home, that my "break" from critical thinking was actually a shift that had brought me to a new relationship with critical thinking. What it means, now, for me to move through critical thinking in my gendered, post-partum body is a genuinely different set of negotiations and affects than it was before. Never mind that my time has become even more confetti-like than ever. No, what I mean is that as a person who writes about affect and poetics—structures and feelings and structures of feelings—my gendered body is even more unavoidable. It is, I daresay, necessary.

Sara Ahmed has written that vulnerability and fragility are places from which feminist work happens:

In so many research projects: you end up enacting what you are accounting for. A fragile thread woven of our fragility. Easily broken.

Fragility: the quality of being easily breakable.[8]

As I sat in the washroom trying quietly to pump and dump milk between panels and to think about the papers I had just heard, I began to realize that the division I try to keep between the "personal" and the "professional"—a false dichotomy if ever there was one—was unnecessary. I was missing a point: these new experiences of fragility offer crucial moments where critical thinking *is* happening. Perception-altering events.

Fragility is a place where crucial feminist work happens. Fragility and sweat. Crucial places where mothering and feminism bruise against each other until I let them coexist.

*

This morning I was standing in the kitchen, making coffee. Bébé was on the other side of the kitchen, looking out the window at our dog in the yard. *Mama!* she said in her small, squeaky voice, *mama! Yes, babe?* I look her way. And there she is, standing on her own two, chubby feet. She takes one step towards me, then two-three-four. *Wow wow wow!* I clap! *Look at you, little goose!* Then she's up on her tiptoes laughing and clapping at her own feat. *Mama! Mama!* She claps and laughs and falls down laughing. *Mama.* That's me.

---

8. Sara Ahmed, "Fragility," *feministkilljoys* 14 Jun 2014 <http://feministkill-joys.com/2014/06/14/fragility/>.

I pick her up and hug her.

Mama! she says.

Yes, babe, that's me! I say.

Yes, that's me.

Postscript:
Sometimes Refusal is a Feminist Act

Refusal. A word that can carry negative connotations of difficulty. Also a word with revolutionary potential. A word that, for me, at least, always brings to mind *Refus Global*. *Refus Global* (or "total refusal," as it translates into English) was a manifesto written and signed by sixteen young people in Quebec in 1948. At that moment in Quebec, private life was structured by the repressive public policies of the Duplessis government (which was, in turn, actively supported by the Catholic Church). The era in which *Refus Global* was written is now known as Grande Noirceur— Great Darkness. It was not a great moment to be a woman or a labour rights activist. And so it is significant that of the sixteen signatories of this document, seven were women. One of those women was Françoise Sullivan. I have this image of Sullivan in my mind: she's dancing with a wild grace, and she's dancing outside in the snow in the middle of winter. That dance, *Danse dans la neige/Dance in Snow, 1947,* was an exploration of the seasons. It remains one of the most significant moments in Canadian art history. I don't know, but I like to imagine that Sullivan's *Danse* was itself a precursor to the creation of *Refus Global*. The document those friends and artists penned called for social change and possibility. History doesn't remember the women of that document as well as it does the men, but let us remember: these women signed a public document calling for radical and revolutionary and freeing change.[1] They signed a document that positioned refusal as a means of imagining other possible worlds. Refusal as a rejection of oppressive systems. Refusal as an act of hope for better futures. Refusal as feminist killjoy act.

*

Sometimes, refusal is a feminist act. Sometimes, a feminist killjoy has not just to call out the so-called joys of patriarchal culture, she has to refuse them, too.

*

While I was in the process of finishing this book, Sara Ahmed resigned from her position at Goldsmiths. She wrote that she had resigned because of the university's failure to meaningfully address systemic sexual harassment on cam-

---

1. Patricia Smart's *Les femmes du Refus Global* (Boréal, 1998) is a significant and vital exemption to the historical forgetting of Madeleine Arbour, Marcelle Ferron, Muriel Guilbault, Louise Renaud, Thérèse Leduc, Françoise Riopelle, and Françoise Sullivan. I am grateful to Pat for her correspondence with me about these women.

pus. Her students published a letter of solidarity with her. This is a significant and monumental move. Tenure—which is a kind of permanent job status—is increasingly difficult to get, as universities stop hiring tenure-track professors and retirements are being replaced less and less. Giving up tenure means giving up security in a system that ensures your pay as well as your ability to do the work you've trained for years to do. Women, women of colour, people of colour, and differently abled people are less likely to get tenured positions than white, English-speaking men who pass as straight. Giving up tenure means giving up a place at the table. It means giving up a space in the system. Resignation as refusal is an act that says the system is broken and I will not participate in the lies that we have to tell or the silences that we have to keep in order to pretend otherwise.

In her own description of her resignation, Ahmed articulates refusal as reaching a point of "feminist snap":

What I had been asked to bear became too much; the lack of support for the work we were doing; the walls we kept coming up against. That I could resign depended upon having material resources and security. But it still felt like I was going out on a limb: I did not just feel like I was just leaving a job, or an institution, but also a life, an academic life; a life I had loved; a life I was used to. And that act of leaving was a form of feminist snap: there was a moment when I couldn't take it anymore, those walls of indifference that were stopping us from getting anywhere; that were stopping us from getting through. Once the bond had snapped, I realised that I had been trying to hold onto something that had already broken… By snapping you are saying: I will not reproduce a world I cannot bear, a world I do not think should be borne.[2]

Feminist Snap—a moment of killjoy refusal. A breaking point. A point at which you break from oppressive and repressive systems.

★

These moments are sometimes quiet, and other times, not. They are almost always public in some way. Refusal as solidarity. Refusal as killjoy praxis. Refusal as a hopeful, world-making gesture.

★

This postscript brings us back to where we started; back to attempts to refuse the so-called joys of patriarchal culture. But back with a difference. That's repetition with a difference: this is a refrain, an eternal return, a perception-altering event.

In order to bring these notes to a kind of close, I want to show you how these threads of feminist killjoy/friend/mother/sometimes-teacher in a university setting have, through the sweaty, laborious work of my bodily thinking, shifted how I understand my relational responsibilities in the world.

---

2. Sara Ahmed, "Speaking Out," *feministkilljoys* 2 Jun 2016 <https://feminist-killjoys.com/2016/06/02/speaking-out/>.

*

Think of the threads as birds flying, wings spread.

*

Think of them as lines of flight.

*

Some years ago, I was teaching a Canadian Studies class. "The Idea of Canada," it was called.

The notion that there could be a singular "idea" troubled me, and I told my students so, breaking down my own privilege for them.

How many of you do a double-take with me standing at the front of the classroom, I asked them. A few tentative hands. *Is it my whiteness?* I asked.

No.

Is it my gender? That I look and sound and act and identify as a cis-gender woman?

No.

Is it my non-descript North American accent?

No, not unless I drop a "y'all," thus betraying a decade-plus of my childhood spent in the rural southern United States.

Is it my tattoos?

Yes, haha—little, careful giggles.

What can we make of this? I asked the students. *That my whiteness, my heteronormativity, my unaccented English make me a relatively expected presence at the front of the classroom?*

Yes.
Yes, they agreed.
Yes, there's something to that.

Okay, I said, *let's unpack these assumptions inscribed on my body. Let's think about power. Let's do that in the context of these lands and ideas called Canada.*

We spent the fall breaking down what "that" might mean, moving through pluralities—lands, stories, narratives, nations, histories, oppositions, solidarities. It was one of those classes in a large amphitheatre, the kind where if you're lecturing at the front you can see everybody in the room, but if you're seated, you feel anonymous.

I would like to tell you every that student was riveted, but that would be a lie.

Instead, there were a few, scattered mainly in the front rows, who became dependable barometers for me.

Lecture going well? M. would be leaning forward in her seat. J. would be nodding and writing notes. Lecture off-track or not engaging? B. would look disappointed.

Late in the semester, we started talking about the gatherings, rallies, and demonstrations that were happening across the country. I was teaching in K'jipuktuk in Mi'kma'ki (Halifax, Nova Scotia) at Dalhousie University. Several of my students in the course self-identified as Indigenous. We talked about how the media was narrativizing these rallies as unprecedented, as springing up from the land as if from nowhere. The wrong stories were being told about the peoples and the reasons for protests, we decided. The general public was being fed half-truths, misrepresentations, and lies.

How lucky, I thought, to have these movements happen now, as we are in this class together, thinking through "Canada" and "Ideas" about it. Something to shift us, maybe. Something teachable, definitely.

The students felt it, too, this thing I'm calling luck, some of them more than others (later, a few course evaluations would say *too much feminism,* or *I didn't think this was going to be a class about Indigenous issues. Or she,* meaning me, *is too political*). The ones who were paying attention—to the news, not necessarily to me—worked to articulate some of the energy they were seeing. What is a round dance? Can I really participate? What is bannock? I was asked these questions after class or in careful, apologetic emails. The apologies to me, the white teacher at the front of the room, gave me pause. I felt a heaviness in my body—an awareness of my responsibility and, more, of my inadequacy.

*

I can't ever remember not being aware of my own body in the world. Specifically, I mean my own gendered body. Even more specifically, I can't remember a time when I haven't been told or taught or intuited that my worth as a body-gendered-female had to do with the space I take up.

*

I started counting calories when I was eleven or twelve.

This was before the Internet, before the circulation of selfies became its own kind of regulatory or freeing tool, depending.

One of my friends explained her lack of snack at recess: *I'm fat*, she said. And I thought, oh, is that something I should worry about, too? This girl, my friend, was more popular than me.

I started noticing that my mom was careful—that's what she called it, *being careful*—with food. She would refuse second helpings, a taste of meat from my father's plate, snacks with *Murder, She Wrote* on Sunday evenings. I can't remember how it came up, but when I asked her about food she told me that women had to be cautious. She gave me a booklet that told you how many calories were in items of food.

I started writing things down. 1,200. That was the magic number. I became good at math, though I was struggling with it in school.

*

It's funny how things change, and how they stay the same.

The first few days and weeks after we brought our girl home, I would write down how long she nursed. In the middle of the night, with this tiny human in my arms, I would type, right side 3:40–4:05 a.m., left side 4:20–4:45 a.m. into the notes app on my phone.

After a week, the midwives came to our house, stripped her down to her diaper, wrapped her in a little cloth sling and measured her in a hand scale.

She looked like she was getting ready for market.

Eight pounds, they pronounced, *good*.

I felt relieved. I stopped logging her nursing quite as obsessively.

And then, one day, I just stopped logging it entirely.

*

In the fall of 2012, Idle No More gained traction across the country. This was around the end of the semester and the completion of my Canadian Studies class.

One day, after classes had ended, I was completing some grading in my office when I received an email from one of my students. It was M. She was working on a press release for an Idle No More gathering in the city and wanted to know if I would read it over. She was on campus, so I walked over to where she was in the First Nations Students' Association. Neither M. nor I had ever written a press release, so I put up a plea on social media, asking for help.

The first person to respond was then-Halifax NDP MP Megan Leslie.

Leslie sent an example and some notes.

She sent it right away.

I need to tell you this, and I need you to hear it: Megan Leslie, whom neither M. nor I had ever met, responded right away.

(Don't get me started on how this woman has been denigrated for her feminism. Don't get me started on her generosity. These are not the same stories, but they both—her feminism, her generosity—require labour from her. She helped us immediately because we asked.)

We circulated the announcement, and later that week I gathered at the first of a series of public meetings about Omnibus Bill C-45. Among other things, C-45 (the Jobs and Growth Act) proposed to overhaul the Navigable Waters Protection Act and to extinguish Canada's duty to consult with First Nations when enacting developments that would affect First Nations' lands and communities.

Lands. Bodies. Nourishment.

That's the whole of what makes us up, isn't it?

These are root issues. Rooting issues.

M.'s sister and another Mi'kmaq woman were the central organizers of the gatherings that were happening across the city and province. When Chief Theresa Spence made her journey from Attawapiskat to Ottawa, when she embarked on her hunger strike, while she waited for the former Prime Minister to concede to meet with her, the women here went on hunger strike in solidarity. At a rally, M.'s sister invited everyone present to consider joining the solidarity hunger strike. I thought about what I could do and whether it would mean anything if I, alone in my home, was quietly striking in solidarity. I decided it meant something to join this struggle viscerally, with my own body. I told M. that

I would join as well. Three days of only water and broth in solidarity with a woman, a chief, sitting across from the Parliament buildings, waiting for the prime minister to speak with her. Waiting, on behalf of her people. Waiting in Ottawa, Algonquin Territory. Waiting, hungry. What is three days of my time, I thought. Me, with my unearned white privilege. Me, with my credentials. Me, with my cisgender. Me, with so much and yet here, on my students' traditional lands, unrooted. From elsewhere (where?).

What is three days when I can show my solidarity with my student, her sister, her community, her histories. What is three days of being hungry. Nothing. Three days is nothing to give another person.

*

Do you understand what I mean by "inadequacy"? This isn't a story about my own self-doubt. I was starting to finally, or again, to feel the weight of colonial violence, of histories of peoples who are not my own, but whose histories are my responsibility to learn.

And I was feeling the weight of the violences that my body already carried. *Do your students always cry in your office, tell you about their traumas, confide in you?* No, not always. But often. My male colleagues would ask me that, mostly.

*

The comments on any news story about Chief Theresa Spence were appalling. They were beyond ignorant; they were wilfully hateful. They were racist and misogynist. Don't read the comments. That should be a given; yet, when you're alone with the Internet, trying to connect with what's happening elsewhere, sometimes you read them. People commented on Spence's weight. News outlets speculated about the validity of her fast. Calories were counted. Upon learning that she was drinking fish broth, the mainstream media renamed Chief Spence's hunger strike a *liquid diet*.

There was, as Leanne Simpson writes, little to no understanding amongst settler-colonial Canada that fish broth is a traditional Anishinabeg survival diet—a diet that emerged as a result of the repercussions of colonial violence.[3] There are many ways to make people hungry, after all.

★

Hate for an Indigenous woman acting on behalf of her community fed more than trolls; it fed the violent monster of colonialism and white imperialism. And at the centre of this verbal violence, a woman—a mother—waited on the banks of the Rideau River, hungry.

★

3. Leanne Simpson, "Fish Broth & Fasting," *Leanne Betasamosake Simpson* 16 Jan 2013 <http://leannesimpson.ca/fish-broth-fasting/>.

Two days after our girl was born, we came home and I showered. I had taken a shower at the hospital almost immediately, but I hardly recall it. I remember asking my partner what was strapped between my legs. It was me, my body, swollen from twenty-four hours of work.

I couldn't stand very well—the epidural left me shaky—and I remember we didn't even try to wash the vomit out of my hair, so hear me when I say that that first shower at home was amazing.

And terrifying. It was terrifying, too. I so vividly remember forcing myself to wash my breasts, which had more than doubled in size and were crisscrossed with purple stretch marks. I recall forcing myself to wash my stomach and abdomen and to say aloud to myself *good job, body*, rather than recoil at its foreignness.

I'm not proud of this, but it is a truth that needs naming. *Good job*, I said, to each part of myself, as I carefully washed. *Good job*. A mantra to teach myself about myself.

*

What was it like for Chief Spence, there, waiting? What is it like for anyone waiting to be acknowledged, waiting to have their needs and the needs of their people acknowledged as real, as meaningful. These stories and questions that intersect.

*

When I was on the second day of the solidarity fast I got a call from a now-defunct rightwing media corporation.

Would I talk about why I was on a hunger strike?

It's not a hunger strike, but yes, I will talk about solidarity and allyship to your viewers.

Yes, I will try.

Better me in those comment sections than my students, I thought. It is my responsibility to try to teach outside my comfort zone.

What a thing, to have a comfort zone.

*

I threw up before the interview—a mix of nerves and headache from not eating.

The interview was less hostile than I'd been expecting.

Why do you think it is important for you to be on hunger strike? asked the disembodied voice.

It's not important for me to be on a hunger strike, I replied, *but it is important for my students to know I stand in solidarity with them outside the classroom as well. And hey, you've given me a platform to speak to your viewers about colonial violence, so that's useful as well. Thank you.*

The interview ended there.

★

When my daughter cries for food my breasts leak, or at least they used to. Now I just check to see if they leak.

They hurt, too. No one tells you that it hurts. Actually, no one told me much of anything physiological until after I gave birth; before then it was all relationship advice, nothing about the body. My body. Then suddenly there were complicit, whispered conversations with other women who had been pregnant and given birth.

I say whispered because people get bored really quickly with hearing about your body, even the people who are closest to you.

Get over it.

That's the look I see—or misinterpret.

Don't let your leaky body or your leaky feelings touch me. Don't take up too much space with your body and its vicissitudes, its oceanic shifts.

*

Lately, I have been trying to think about how the space I take up physically—as a settler, as a woman living in a patriarchal system—is related to using and occupying space, to regulating and controlling access to space.

I have been thinking about how my body has been complicit in the regulation of other bodies, and how my body has learned self-surveillance.

I have been thinking about my baby, here in these spaces for the first time.

How do I teach her about respect, while making sure she knows that she deserves it, too?

How do I teach her that her body is her own?

How do I teach her reciprocity and kindness?

How do I teach her to share her water if a person is thirsty?

How do I teach her to refuse a culture that suggests she shouldn't share her water if a person is thirsty?

*

Water. The right to access safe and clean water in a country made of lakes and rivers and streams and ponds. That's part of what Omnibus Bill C-45 was about—restricting those rights, and especially the rights of Indigenous peoples.

⋆

We dipped our girl in the ocean first. The Northumberland Strait, to be exact. Later, we dipped her in Gull Lake. She held her little naked body perfectly straight and looked up at us, blinking.

⋆

Refusal is a feminist act when you are acting in solidarity. Refusal is a feminist act when you are acting against the oppression of others. Refusal is a feminist act when you kill the so-called joys of patriarchal culture.

Refusal is a feminist act when you forge new lines of flight— away from what is into what might be.

Acknowledgements

To all feminist killjoys fighting for unfetterd joy and against oppression.

To Jay and Hazel for their trust.

To Tanya Murphy and Paul Henderson and Graeme Patterson and Amanda Fauteaux, for helping me to articulate my vision in design language.

To Hannah McGregor and Hannah Moscovitch and Rebecca Blakey and Joanna Erdman, for helping me think through sections of the writing here. All mistakes are, of course, mine and not theirs.

To Shannon Webb-Campbell and Lucia Lorenzi and Melissa Dalgleish. Brilliant minds and rebellious mermaids, all.

To Susan Bennett and Carrie Dawson and Laura Moss and Christina Luckyj and Marjorie Stone and Jade Ferguson and Linda Morra: mentors and friends and inspirations, all.

To the humans of CWILA: Canadian Women in the Literary Arts, working for representational justice in Canadian literary culture.

To the humans of *Hook & Eye: Fast Feminism, Slow Academe*, for being comrades, friends, and fierce writers.

To the humans of *GUTS Canadian Feminist Magazine*, for letting me republish a version of "The Space We Take Up," which they published first. To Cynthia Spring, for encouraging me to write it in the first place, and for editing it so wisely and generously.

To Natalie Childs and Caitrin Redmond, for loving our bébé and giving her care.

To Jerry Ropson and Katie Lo, for loving our bébé and being chosen family to her.

To Julie Joosten, magical talented editor extraordinaire, for gently and carefully and patiently pulling this book out of me & making it better than I could have imagined.

To Catherine Bryan, for dancing wildly in the kitchen with me always.

To my parents and my Aunt Mary Lou, for supporting me even (& especially) when you might not agree.

To Nancy Sanford and Emily Sanford, for their expansive hearts and boundless support.

To my heart's hearts: B. & E. My loves. My family. My home I hoped for. Thank you for making worlds with me.

& once more, to B., for talking, for thinking with me, for careful editing in the wee hours before deadlines, and for moving through the world with a genuine ethics of care. You inspire and delight me daily.

& finally, & utterly: for bébé.

Colophon

Distributed in Canada by the Literary Press Group:
www.lpg.ca

Distributed in the United States by Small Press Distribution:
www.spdbooks.org

Shop online at www.bookthug.ca

Essais are edited for the press by Julie Joosten
Designed by Malcolm Sutton
Typeset in Dante
Copy edited by Ruth Zuchter

BOOK
PRODUCTION
WAR ECONOMY
STANDARD